I AM

Names, Divine Attributes,
and
Characteristics of Jehovah

Pastor Rudo smith 10/11/23

Evangelist Richard Mattock

Jer 29:11

For I Know The plans I Have For
you - Plans To prosper you And not
to harm you. Plans To give
you Hope And A future

WESTBOW
P R E S S®
A DIVISION OF THOMAS NELSON
& ZONDERVAN

Scripture taken from the King James Version of the Bible.

Scripture taken from the New King James Version®. Copyright © 1982 by Thomas Nelson. Used by permission. All rights reserved.

Scripture taken from The Message. Copyright © 1993, 1994, 1995, 1996, 2000, 2001, 2002. Used by permission of NavPress Publishing Group.

Scripture taken from the Amplified Bible, Copyright © 1954, 1958, 1962, 1964, 1965, 1987 by The Lockman Foundation. Used with permission.

Scripture taken from The One New Man Bible, copyright © 2011 William J. Morford. Used by permission of True Potential Publishing, Inc.

THE HOLY BIBLE, NEW INTERNATIONAL VERSION®, NIV® Copyright © 1973, 1978, 1984, 2011 by Biblica, Inc.® Used by permission. All rights reserved worldwide.

WestBow Press books may be ordered through booksellers or by contacting:

WestBow Press
A Division of Thomas Nelson & Zondervan
1663 Liberty Drive
Bloomington, IN 47403
www.westbowpress.com
1 (866) 928-1240

ISBN: 978-1-9736-0982-7 (sc)
ISBN: 978-1-9736-0984-1 (hc)
ISBN: 978-1-9736-0983-4 (e)

Library of Congress Control Number: 2017917300

Print information available on the last page.

WestBow Press rev. date: 11/07/2017

Acknowledgments

Pastor/Teacher Doctor All Brice—Covenant Love Church Fayetteville
North Carolina
Gideon Mighty Man of Valor... 73-76
King Asa... 91-94
Hope sees through the darkness... 180-182
Rejoicing Father... 221-224

Foreword

"The primary question in a Christian's life is that of, how do I know God? In Church we talk about God continually. Christian faith claims to have knowledge of God—not fantasy, imagination, or guesswork, but knowledge." That is very important because God said in Hosea 4:6a...My people are destroyed for lack of knowledge. If I don't have the knowledge of who God is, then I will never understand how He thinks about me, how He loves me, how can He help me, and simply, who is He to me as His child in a covenant relationship. Without this knowledge, I become a weak believer with a very impotent belief system that the devil will exploit constantly.

Richard Mattock has been a long time member at Covenant Love Church, a diligent student of God's Word, and an anointed Evangelist. He has written an intensive and comprehensive book on the Names of God. Daniel 11:32b states, but the people who know their God shall be strong, and carry out great exploits. If you desire to go to a deeper level of knowing God, discover the greatness of your God, be a fearless believer, and see your faith soar to new heights, then you must read and study this book. It is a believer's spiritual warfare manual for these last days. If you don't know the Redemptive and Covenant Names of God, then how will you walk and be victorious against the Kingdom of Darkness? Jesus walked in victory because He knew who His Father God was, how about you? Ready to do great exploits for the Kingdom, then fill your heart and renew your mind by reading "I AM". God Bless

Dr Al Brice
Sr Pastor Covenant Love Church

Contents

III. The Name of God Almighty—El Shaddai—Almighty God

IV. God the Master Potter

V. God Likes You

VI. Who Will Pray for the Peace of Jerusalem?

Introduction

How Important Are the Names of God?

Our Father, Who art in Heaven, Hallowed be Thy Name … God's name is to be hallowed, sanctified, consecrated, made holy, set apart not just in our heads but in our hearts. When we pray "Hallowed be Thy Name," we are acknowledging God as holy. We are choosing to reverence and to exalt the name that speaks of His eternal character. All God's attributes are everlasting, so we must always begin our prayers and our cries for assistance by focusing on God's great names.

The reason for studying the names of God is to know God. The more we know God, the more confidence we will have that God will do what He said He would do.

"The people who know their God shall be strong, and carry out great exploits (heroic acts)" (Daniel 11:32 NKJV). We can increase our faith by learning more about God. Who has great faith? People who have great knowledge of God.

By the names of God, we mean all those attributes through which He is revealed to us—His love, power, wisdom, holiness, justice, and truth among them.

Discovering the majesty of who God is in all His glory and majesty enables us to more fully comprehend our relationship with Him as our Creator. "Great is the Lord, and greatly to be praised; and his greatness is unsearchable" (Psalm 145:3 NKJV).

Instead of allowing our lives to be confined to our limited view of whom we think God is, we must humble ourselves and see Him as He has revealed Himself to us through scripture.

> And they shall not teach every man his neighbor, and every man his brother, saying, Know the Lord: for all shall know me, from the least to the greatest. (Hebrews 8:11)

One of God's greatest desires for us as His people is for us to know Him as He reveals Himself throughout the scriptures and discover who He is and His special, divine characteristics that make Him the majestic God He is. We were created in His image, which enables us to personally experience His divine attributes. We must keep in mind that these attributes are least understood through our intellect and best known through faith.

What's in a Name?

Our society places little significance on the meaning of a name, but names do indeed mean things: Kenneth means "to know," Philadelphia means "brotherly love," Jerusalem means "city of peace," Christ means "the anointed one," and Immanuel means "God is with us."

Names often provide information regarding the nature of a person or place. The Bible refers to God by many names based on His character or His relationship with us. While some people use God's name in prayer, others use His name in cursing, which shows only how little they know God. If those who curse in God's name really knew Him, they would know He said, "Thou shall not take the name of the Lord in vain, for the Lord will not hold him guiltless that taketh his name in vain" (Exodus 20:7). For over two hundred years, people did not call on God by name. It wasn't until the birth of Adam's grandson Enos that "men began to call upon the name of the Lord" (Genesis 4:26).

God explained to Moses that He had appeared to Abraham, Isaac, and Jacob. Moses was given the task of returning to Egypt and demanding the release of the Israelite slaves. Moses asked God, "When I come unto the children of Israel and shall say unto them, the God of your fathers hath sent me unto thee, and they say to me, what is his name, what shall I say unto them?" Perhaps Moses wanted to know God's name because the name would tell him something about God. God said unto Moses, "I AM that I AM. I AM has sent me unto you" (Exodus 3:13–14). He said His name was "I Am."

I Am

Holy, Creator, the Most-High God, Righteous, Joy, Peace, Lord Mighty in Battle, God of the Battle, Conquer, High Tower and Strong Tower, Defender, Deliver, thy Strength, thy Sword, thy Shield, your Rock, the Wine, your Fortress, your Refuge, Shepherd, Kingsman Redeemer, Jubilee, Horn of thy Salvation, Sanctifier, Love, Mercy, Grace, Hope, Provider, Healer, Omnipresent, Omnipotent, Judge, and Jealous.

There are covenant names of Jehovah and redemptive names through which God revealed Himself to Israel. These names do not signify forty different Gods but His characteristics and attributes.

The Name of Jehovah

And I appeared unto Abraham, unto Isaac, and unto Jacob, by the name of God Almighty, but by my name JEHOVAH was I not known unto them. (Exodus 6:3)

A full revelation of the meaning and character of the name Jehovah is not given by God until Exodus 3:14: God said to Moses, "I AM THAT I AM" and He said, "Thus you shall say to the sons of Israel, 'I AM has sent me to you.'"

In Exodus 3:15, God told Moses

Thus, you shall say to the sons of Israel, The LORD, the God of your fathers, the God of Abraham, the God of Isaac, and the God of Jacob, has sent me to you. This is My Name forever, and this is My Memorial-Name to all generations.

Does God Have a Proper Name?

Most Bible scholars agree that the name Yahweh, or Jehovah, as it is sometimes translated, would be the proper name of God. The other names, including the compound names, provide further revelation of His character and activity.

I: Seven Redemptive Names of Jehovah

1. Jehovah Jireh—The Lord Will Provide

In the hour when Abraham's faith was to be tested, God revealed one of His names—Jehovah Jireh. With a knife in his hand, Abraham told his son that God would provide a lamb for a burnt offering.

> Abraham stretched forth his hand, and took the knife to slay his son, and behold behind him a ram caught in a thicket by his horns: and Abraham went and took the ram, and offered him up for a burnt offering in the stead of his son. And Abraham called the name of that place **Jehovah Jireh**. (Genesis 22:10, 13)

The Lord will provide. They learned that God was the provider of all they needed. He had provided the Lamb that all humanity would need for sacrifice.

They could have possibly seen the Hill of Golgotha, where Jesus Christ would offer His life as a sacrifice for humanity's sins. This was where King Solomon offered animal sacrifices.

Jehovah-Jireh is one of the many names of God in the Old Testament. The story begins with a command from God to Abraham to sacrifice his son of promise as a burnt offering. The next morning, Abraham took a knife, and he and Isaac traveled to Moriah, the place God had chosen.

As they neared the site, Isaac questioned Abraham concerning the intended offering: "Where is the lamb?" Abraham replied, "God himself will provide the lamb for the burnt offering, my son" (Genesis 22:8). The New Testament tells us that Abraham believed God would raise Isaac from the dead (Hebrews 11:19).

Abraham demonstrated his faith and obedience by building an altar and placing Isaac on the wood. Before Abraham could finish offering his son, the angel of the Lord called to him from heaven, and Isaac's life was spared. Abraham saw a ram caught by its horns in a thicket; he sacrificed it instead of his son (Genesis 22:14). Abraham named the place Jehovah-Jireh because of God's gracious provision of a substitute for Isaac.

Immediately afterward, God reconfirmed His covenant with Abraham. Centuries later, King Solomon built a temple there. The account of Abraham on Mount Moriah is a dramatic illustration of faith and obedience and a presentation of the Lord's continual provision.

The statement "on the mountain of the LORD it will be provided" (Genesis 22:14) refers to more than Mount Moriah—it also refers to a hill called Calvary, where God did not spare His Son but gave Him up for us all.

Watch the Birds

> Take no thought for your life, what ye shall eat, or what you shall drink: nor yet for your body, what you shall put on. Is not the life more than meat, and the body than rainment? Behold the fowls (BIRDS) of the air: For they sow not, neither do they reap nor gather into barns, yet your Heavenly Father feedeth them. Are you not more better than they? (Matthew 6:25–26)

Learning from the Birds

The Lord said, "Consider the fowls of the air. That we are much better than they, but the Heavenly Father feedeth them and provides for them."

I'll start worrying when I see birds building barns. But you don't see them building barns, because they know God will take care of them. The world is full of anxieties and fears. Why can't we read this verse, consider the birds, and see how they respond? You don't see them going around worrying whether God will take care of them.

Little Birds

Once when I was in a building, I heard a loud racket. It sounded like a bunch of little birds going crazy every time their mother showed up. I saw her chew a bug or worm so they could digest it. What dawned on me was what causes this mother to come back to this nest—the love of the Father.

Like the tiny birds, we should cry out so all will know they have been blessed by their heavenly Father. We need to consider the birds and trust that God will provide!

What the Bible Teaches Us

On the night HE was betrayed, Jesus asked HIS disciples, "when I sent you out without purse, and scrip, and shoes, lacked ye anything?" And they said nothing. God provided the food, clothing, and money these first evangelists needed. (Luke 22:35)

But my God shall supply all my need according to His riches in glory by Christ Jesus. (Philippians 4:19)

Seek ye first the kingdom of God and His righteousness; and all these things shall be added unto you. When we put God first, then HE will become our provider. (Matthew 6:33)

> I have been young, and now am old; yet have I not seen
> the righteous forsaken nor HIS seed begging bread.
> (Psalm 37:25)

Remembering His Benefits

> Bless the Lord, O my soul, and all that is within me, Bless
> his Holy Name. Bless the Lord, O my soul, and forget not
> all his benefits. Who forgiveth all thine iniquities; who
> healeth all thy diseases. (Psalm 103:1–3)

There are many benefits to serving the Lord, but the most important is having our sins forgiven and our diseases healed.

> And the Lord said unto Abram, after Lot was separated
> from him, lift up now your eyes, and look from the place
> where thou art northward, and southward, and eastward,
> and westward: For all the land, which thou see to thee
> will I give it, and to thy seed forever. (Genesis 13:14–15)

The Word of God tells us He has made great and precious promises to us. God wants everyone to experience all He has provided in His Word.

Here are three major truths that will help us to enter into our inheritance.

1. See

To see is to know what God has promised and made available to us. We must know what is available to us before we will ever experience it. The problem today is spiritual ignorance; we are ignorant of what God has provided for us.

In Genesis 13:14–15, God told Abraham "to lift up your eyes (enlarge your vision). Look to the north, south, east, and west. All the Land that you see I will give to you."

Lift up your eyes and look from.

Lift up your eyes and look to.

Lift up your eyes and look now.

What you see is what you get.

Lift up now thine eyes, and look from the place where thou art. Body of Christ, look from where you are even if you are experiencing the good things of God. It becomes dangerous to dwell on where you are; you can become stagnant and nearsighted.

Many Christians want to stay the way they are, but there are more and greater things God wants to do for them. Maybe your situation is bad—sickness, poverty, and fear—and you feel you can't take it anymore. Your situation may be terrible, but it's subject to change.

Get away from the poor "Oh my" attitude. You hear people say, "Nobody has been as sick as me" or "Nobody has had it as tough as me." Oh yes, you may have it rough, but lift up your eyes from where you are.

> There hath no temptation taken you but such is common
> to man: But God is faithful, who will not suffer you to
> be tempted above that you are able: but will with the
> temptation also make a way to escape, that you may be
> able to bear it. (Corinthians 10:13)

You may have it horrible, you may have it bad, but Satan is not able to come up with something new. Stop looking at where you are; that keeps you from experiencing God's best in your life. "Lift up now thine eyes, and look from the place where thou art, and looking to Jesus, the author and finisher of our faith" (Hebrews 12:2).

Look to Jesus

How do I do that? Jesus said, "I and my Word are one." I look to the Word about my situation and not at the situation.

You may say I am poor; the Word says He became poor that you might become rich.

You may say I am sick; the Word says that by His stripes you were healed.

Lift up your eyes and get things in the now. That's the problem with Christians today;

they never get things in the now. Look to Jesus and His promises.

To see it will not automatically mean you will experience it (Numbers 13:26–33). "But nevertheless, the people be strong that dwell in the land" (Numbers 13:28). Two groups saw the same thing, but it wasn't what they saw but how they saw it. Joshua and Caleb saw what God said; the other ten spies saw circumstances. Until we believe what God says and resist the lies of Satan, we will remain beholder rather than holder.

The more they talked, the worse it got. They began to magnify it. They began to put thoughts there that weren't real. They all were not giants. They made a mountain out of an anthill. First, they said it was a land flowing with milk and honey, then they said it was a land that ate its inhabitants. "It's a bad land," they said, yet they had it in their hands.

They turned against Moses; the whole congregation said they'd have been better off staying in Egypt. Christians say the same thing when things get bad: "I was better before I became a Christian."

Joshua said, "Let's go at once and possess the land; the more talk, the more doubt and unbelief." They didn't make it to the Promised Land as God said because they wouldn't believe God. If God tells you something and it doesn't come to pass, it's because you did not believe Him. God said in Numbers 14 that if you did not take possession of what belonged to you, you were despising it and you would bear your unbelief and disobedience and your carcass would be wasted in the wilderness.

What you say is what you can have. If God said it, you can have it. Caleb said we could do it because God said the land was ours. Joshua said, "Let us go at once and possess the land because the Lord is with us."

2. Take

When they got there, they had to fight, but they won when they did what God said. The violent take it by force (Matthew 11:12). One who is aggressive knows what is his and takes what belongs to him. He fights the good fight of faith, not physical.

> And it came to pass, when David and his men were come to Ziklag on the third day, that the Amalekites had

invaded the South, and Ziklag, and smitten Ziklag, and burned it with fire.

And had taken the women captives, that were therein: they slew not any, either great or small, but carried them away, and went on their way. So, David and his men came to the city, and behold, it was burned with fire, and their wives, and their sons, and their daughters, were taken captives. Then David and the people that were with him lifted up their voice and wept, until they had no more power to weep. And David inquired at the Lord, saying, shall I pursue after this troop? Shall I overtake them? And he answered him, pursue: for thou shall surely overtake them, and without fail recover all. (1 Samuel 30:1–4, 8)

Every Christian Is Called to Warfare

The weapons of our warfare are not carnal but are mighty and can pull down all strongholds. Our weapons of warfare are the nine gifts of the Spirit, the whole armor of God, the precious blood of Jesus Christ, and the name of Jesus.

Peter and John said to the lame man, "In the name of Jesus Christ arise and walk" (Acts 3-6). "Thy name is an ointment poured forth" (Song of Solomon 1:3). "For thy name is near thy wondrous works declared" (Psalm 75:1).

The blood of Jesus reminds demons of their defeat and coming Judgment. The followers of Jesus overcame the devil by their testimony and the blood of the Lamb.

Engaging the throne room of God with praise and thanksgiving so God will arise and enemies will be scattered. When God rises, the dead things in your life are raised by His power. God has given us all talents; the problem with the man who buried his one talent is that he compared himself with those who had received more talents. When you compare yourself with somebody else, some of your anointing, your future, your testimony, and your power is buried because of comparison, intimidation, fear, or compromise. "I can't sing like her." "I can't preach like him."

Whatever the enemy has dared to bury can be miraculously raised by the risen Christ.

3. Hold

Hold fast to whatever you have.

- That which is good (1 Thessalonians 5:21)
- The form of sound words (2 Timothy 4:2)
- Your confession (Hebrews 4:14)
- What you have (Revelation 3:11)

King of Assyria

> For he said, by the strength of my hand I have done it, and by my wisdom; for I am prudent: and I HAVE REMOVED THE BOUNDS OF THE PEOPLE, AND HAVE ROBBED THEIR TREASURES, and I have put down the inhabitants like a valiant man:
>
> And my hand HATH FOUND THE RICHES OF THE PEOPLE: and as one gathers eggs that are left, THERE WAS NONE THAT MOVED THE WING, NOR OPENED THE MOUTH, OR PEEPED. (Isaiah 10:13–14)

Satan's Boast, King of Assyria

I have removed the bounds of the people; I have robbed their treasures.

His Findings

I have found as a nest the riches of the people, and I began to steal from that nest full of treasures.

His Amazement

It never moved a wing or opened its mouth to peep. It gave no resistance as its nest was robbed. Beloved, don't just sit there and do nothing when he reaches for your treasures. Take up the sword of the Spirit. If you just sit back and do nothing, he will take everything.

Though the Israelites entered the Promised Land, they still faced opposition. Israel was in Canaan experiencing defeats. Canaan is not a type of heaven; it is a type of your life on earth. When you get to heaven, you won't have any more battles.

> In the days of Shamgar the son of Anath, in the days of Jael, the highways were unoccupied, and the travelers walked through byways. The inhabitants of the villages ceased in Israel, until that I Deborah arose, that I arose a mother in Israel. (Judges 5:6–7)

This was going on in the Promised Land.

- God's people were terrified to walk on the highways.
- They walked in fear, carrying unnecessary loads.
- They saw the enemy coming and they would run.

Shammah

> And after him was Shammah the son of Agee the Hararite. And the Philistines were gathered together in a troop, where was a piece of ground full of lentils: and the people fled from the Philistines. But he stood in the midst of the ground, and defended it, and slew the Philistines: And the Lord wrought a great victory. (2 Samuel 23:11–12)

He got tired of being ripped off. The others fled, but Shammah stayed. And the Lord brought victory! There has to come a time when you say, "Enough, devil! You pushed me around long enough. This is mine. God gave me the Promised Land. He gave me His Word."

2. Jehovah Nissi—The Lord Is Our Conqueror

> Moses built an altar and called the name of it Jehovah-Nissi, the Lord is Conqueror. For he said; because I will have war with Amalek from generation to generation. (Exodus 17:15–16)

Moses used this name to declare that God would always conquer the enemies of His people. So long as they obeyed the Lord, they would have victory. Moses learned that when he believed God, he conquered.

God has always mastered in making a way where there seemed to be none. God doesn't always work the way we want Him to work, but He said, "Call on me and I will answer thee, and show thee great and mighty things" (Jeremiah 33:3).

In Exodus 3:8, God said, "I AM come down to deliver you out of your affliction." Some of you are being afflicted. You are in a battle, and Satan is fighting you tooth and nail. The devil is your enemy. Jesus said, "The thief cometh not but to steal and to kill and destroy."

I am glad to report to you that God is greater than anyone. If God is for you, no one can be against you. If God is on your side, you cannot lose. If God is standing with you, you will make it through your darkest hours, your hardest trials, and your greatest temptations.

God stated in Exodus 3:1, "I will bring you out." When God tells you He will bring you out, believe it. God will stand by you. He will step in and fight for you.

Going out of Egypt

The children of Israel had been in bondage for over 430 years. When Moses and Aaron requested that they go out to the wilderness and worship God, Pharaoh got so mad with them that he made them work even harder, beat them, and showed them who was boss.

While they were making bricks from mud, they prayed to God. God came on the scene and said, "I have surely seen your affliction and I have heard your prayers and I Am come down to fight your battle for you."

The God of battles stepped down and said, "Egypt, you may be big, you may be powerful, and you may have a lot of wealth. But when I speak, something is going to give."

The God we serve knows how to put the devil on the run.

I am reminded of what the Lord told the children of Israel, two million strong, who marched out of Egypt without drawing a sword. Egypt was so glad to get rid of them after all the plagues that they gave them their jewels, silver, and gold. The Israelites spoiled (striped) the Egyptians. God brought them out with His mighty hand because he was the God of Battles, Jehovah Nissi—the Lord is our Victor.

Israel Left Egypt

A great cloud represented the presence of God. It sat upon the Holy of Holies. It would arise and move. Whenever the watchers saw this cloud moving, they blew their trumpets.

The children of Israel come up to the Red Sea. It's at full tide, and they can't get across. They're standing there and murmuring a lot as we do when things look impossible. If something doesn't happen at the drop of a hat, we get mad and say, "See? God can't do anything for me." Some complained, "He got us through before, but I don't see how He can get us through this one." That's the attitude many Christians have. Moses, however, wasn't worried. Sometimes, we need to be reminded. Moses said, "We came out of Egypt and didn't fire a shot, surely God didn't bring us this far to die in the wilderness. God will make a way; He will see us through."

They stood there with mountains on both sides and Pharaoh's army coming. They got to singing the blues: "There weren't graves in Egypt! You should have left us alone, Moses, making slush and mud." But God wanted to bring them out of that just as He wants to bring you out of your troubles and show you He will fight for you.

Here comes Pharaoh's army. It's dark. They can't see anything. In the Old Testament, God was a pillar of fire by night and a cloud by day.

That pillar of fire was leading them. Everywhere that pillar of fire went, they went.

"Let God arise, let His enemies be scattered," Moses would sing out, and the watchers would blow the trumpets and sound the alarm. That pillar of fire led them to the Red Sea and between two mountains, but Pharaoh's army was behind them. They were led to a place that seemed impossible to escape.

All of a sudden, the light in front of them went over their heads, over two million people, and cast a light over the Red Sea. It was light to the children of Israel, but it was a hindrance to Pharaoh's army. God wanted them to see the miracle; God doesn't hide what He does. Yes, He will do for you as He has done for others. Moses said, "Stand still and see the salvation of the Lord." We need to stand still and watch the light.

The movie *The Ten Commandments* that had them crossing with water lapping around their feet is wrong. The Bible says they crossed on dry ground. I believe the wind dried out a major highway. Someone said it was just a footpath about four feet wide. Do you realize how long it would have taken two million people to walk single file down that path? They might have still been walking! But they got across in one night—two million of them. Scholars say that for them to have crossed in one night, God would have had to have opened a path five miles wide.

The water was as still as Jell-O because the God of Battles spoke. Natural things become unnatural when God speaks. The devil will tell you it won't work, but God said, "I AM going to bring you out."

The children of Israel got through and saw Pharaoh's army; they were fearful. God spoke to the wind, and it ceased; the waters fell on the Egyptians. While they drowned, the children of Israel beat tambourines and sang.

We're passing through the Red Sea; we're heading to that city, to a land that flows with milk and honey. God will see us through. We may find ourselves fighting against all odds or many people, but He's the God of Battles.

What the Bible Teaches Us

Be strong and courageous, be not afraid nor dismay for the King of Assyria, nor for all the multitude that is with him: for there be more with us than with him: For with him is an arm of flesh; for with us is the Lord our God to help us, AND TO FIGHT OUR BATTLES. And the people rested upon the words of Hezekiah King of Judah. (2 Chronicles 32:7–8)

Ah Lord God! Behold, you have made the Heaven and the earth by your great power and stretched out arm, and there is nothing too hard for you: You show loving kindness unto thousands, and recompense the iniquity of the fathers into the bosom of their children after them: THE GREAT, THE MIGHTY GOD, THE LORD OF HOSTS-(WARFARE) IS HIS NAME. (Jeremiah 32:17–18)

Then said David to the Philistine, you come to me with sword, and with a spear, and with a shield, but I come to you in the name of the LORD OF HOSTS-(WARFARE), the God of the armies of Israel, whom you defiled. This day will the Lord deliver you into my hand; and I will smite you, and take your head from you, and I will give the carcasses of the host of the Philistines this day unto the fowls of the air, and to the wild beasts of the earth; that all the earth may know that there is a God in Israel. And all this assembly shall know that the Lord saves not with sword and spear: FOR THE BATTLE IS THE LORD'S, and he will give you unto our hands. (1 Samuel 17:45–47)

David and Goliath

When David went out to fight, he didn't argue the point that Goliath was a huge giant covered from head to toe with armor; he just said that the same God who had helped him battle the lion and the bear would put this uncircumcised Philistine in his hands.

David didn't walk around and say, "I'm worried." He walked out there and said, "God will deliver you into my hands this day because you have defiled the God of the armies of Israel. I will smite thee, and take off your head, and I will give your carcasses to the fowls of the air, and to the wild beasts." We need to make proclamations of what God will do. David knew God would stand by him; he didn't care how big his opponent was. He didn't care he was outnumbered. He knew that when God sent you out to battle, He'd be with you.

Goliath cursed David by his gods. He said, "I take you like a stick and throw you to the dogs," but look what happened. Goliath came toward him, and David picked up five smooth stones. If David had had such faith, why did he pick up five stones instead of just one? David must have heard that Goliath had four big brothers, and David wanted to take care of them too.

We need to be able to stand against the wiles of the devil, and God, who is on our side, will fight our battles. Israel won the victory because God fought the battle.

King Jehoshaphat

> Be not afraid nor dismayed by reason of this great multitude: FOR THE BATTLE IS NOT YOURS BUT GOD'S. (2 Chronicles 20:15)

> Ye shall not need to fight in this battle; set yourselves, stand ye still, and see the salvation of the Lord. (2 Chronicles 20:17)

> And when they began to sing and to praise, the Lord set ambushments. (2 Chronicles 20:22)

They were all destroyed as they turned on each other. An army committed suicide. There was confusion in the camp. Praise confuses the enemy. Judah was not shaking in its boots; that must have been hard on its enemies. They came out praising the Lord.

Elisha Strikes the Syrians Blind (2 Kings 6:13–18)

This king said, "If I get rid of the prophet, I'll get rid of the trouble." He sent a Syrian army after him, and they surrounded the city. If this had been some of us, we would have said, "Surely, this is the end!" and we would have been chewing our fingernails in terror.

One nervous servant came in as white as a ghost and said, "We better get out of here. They have us completely surrounded!" That reminds me of the time the Lone Ranger and Tonto were surrounded by Indians. The Lone Ranger said, "We're surrounded!" Tonto replied, "What do you mean 'we,' paleface?"

The man of God got down and prayed, "God, open my servant's eyes."

He walked out, and for the first time, he saw the angelic host of God. He said, "There are more on our side than there are on their side." He wasn't sweating anymore. He joined the prophet again.

God, open the church's eyes. Help us see there are more on our side then on theirs.

Did you know angelic beings are surrounding us right now? The Bible says that the "Angel of the Lord encamped about them that fear Him."

Our God Will Fight for Us

> In what place, therefore ye hear the sound of the trumpet, resort ye thither unto us: our God shall fight for us. (Nehemiah 4:20)

Take your positions and watch God.

Legion (Mark 5:1–9)

Jesus was in the country of Gadarenes. A man came out from among the tombs. He had been bound many times with chains, but he had broken the chains; no one could tame him. But he met the Lion Tamer. He ran out, fell on his knees, and yelled. Jesus asked him, "Devil, what is your name?" The demons cried out, "We are Legion, for we are many."

It could have been 6,000 or more. The Roman legion in that man's soul was saying, "Jesus, you're outnumbered. I got you surrounded. There's nothing you can do. There's only one of you, Jesus."

But as they were on their way back to hell, they said to Satan, "He's got more power than all of us put together! He said to us to get out, so we had to leave." Jesus's name has enough power to deliver you from whatever you're facing; the God of Battles is on your side.

Seven Sons of Seeva

The sons of Seeva laid hands on a man possessed by demons, but they didn't have any power. The demon said, "Jesus I know, and Paul I know, but who are you?"

Let me tell you that you are somebody if Jesus is in you; the devil knows that Jesus knows how to fight.

Peter Locked Up—James Killed

"Lord hath sent his angel, and he hath delivered me." I can almost hear hell hollering, "Herod has just beheaded James. We got Peter here locked up. We're going to shut the church down!" But little did they know that a handful of people knew the God of Battles and were praying.

Peter was in prison fast asleep. How many of us would be sleeping if we knew we were going to lose our heads the next day? We wouldn't be able to sleep; we'd be pacing all night. But Peter was asleep. The angel had to wake him up. The angel said, "Get up and put on your sandals." He walked up out of that prison because he served the God of Battles.

There's no chain too big, no prison too strong, no river too wide, no fire too hot, no lion too fierce that God cannot handle.

An Atheist and a Gnat

A person who did not believe in God stood on a mountain and tried to defy this God of Battles. "If there be a God, let Him come down and fight with me." While he was standing there, a little gnat flew down his windpipe and choked him to death. God can put your enemies to flight with just a gnat.

A woman testified in church once that she was sitting on her porch when a hornet got right in her face. She was highly allergic to them. Evidently, the hornet was attracted to her perfume, and she cried out, "God, please move this hornet." In a split second, a big, beautiful butterfly moved that hornet out of her face.

No matter how big or small the mountain is, God will fight it for you.

3. Jehovah Ralph—The Lord Who Heals

> Then He proved them, and said, "If thou wilt diligently hearken to the voice of the Lord thy God, and will do that which is right in His sight, and will give ear to His commandments, and keep all His statutes, I will put none of these diseases upon thee, which I have brought upon the Egyptians: For I AM the Lord that Healeth thee." (Exodus 15:26)

They forgot that God was supplying their needs. They failed to read the conditions, and they started complaining. So the Lord allowed fiery serpents to attack their camp. Many were bitten and died.

Moses made them a brass serpent. The Israelites were to look at it and be healed. We too are to look unto Jesus and receive healing.

> Surely He has borne our griefs, and carried our sorrows: yet we did esteem Him stricken, smitten of God, and afflicted. (He suffered in our stead, as our substitute, should have been us) (Isaiah 53:4–5)

These griefs and sorrows indicate disease, sickness, physical and mental oppression. "But He was wounded for our transgressions, He was bruised for our iniquities: the chastisement of our peace was upon Him; and with His stripes we are healed." He suffered for our sin. He took up our infirmities and carried our diseases, so there is no need for us to carry them.

What the Bible Teaches Us

> Bless the Lord, O my soul: and all that is within me, bless His Holy name, and forget not all His benefits. Who forgives all your iniquities; WHO HEALS ALL YOUR

DISEASES. WHO REDEEMS YOUR LIFE FROM
DESTRUCTION. (Psalm 103:1–5)

Jesus never refused to heal anyone. If it had been God's will for people
to be sick, God would have been disappointed with Jesus because he spent
a quarter of His ministry healing the sick.

Sickness Is an Oppression of the Devil

God anointed Jesus of Nazareth with the Holy Ghost and
with power: Who went about doing good, and healing all
that were oppressed of the Devil; for God was with HIM.
(Acts 10:38)

Sickness comes from the devil. God is the source of everything good;
Satan is the source of everything evil. "The thief cometh not but to kill,
steal, and destroy. I am come that they might have life abundantly." (John
10:10) God wants His children to prosper and be in good health just as
their souls prosper. Sickness is not the will of God but the will of the devil.

So, Satan went forth from the presence of God the Lord
and smote Job with boils. (Job 2:7)

Ought not this woman being a daughter of Abraham
whom Satan hath bound, lo, these eighteen years, be
loosed from this bond on the Sabbath day. (Luke 13:16)

How Fallen Angels Afflict Human Beings

- body sores (Job 2:7)
- deafness and dumbness (Matthew 9:32–33)
- physical defects (Luke 13:11–16)
- insanity (Matthew 4:24)
- blindness (Matthew 12:22)
- grievous vexation (Matthew 15:22)

- suicide (Mark 9:22)
- personal injuries (Mark 9:18)
- fever (Luke 4:39)
- epilepsy (Matthew 17:15–18)
- immorality, unclean spirits (Matthew 10:1)
- sickness and disease (Matthew 4:23)

Jesus in His earthly ministry always treated sin, diseases, and devils the same—He rebuked them all.

Jesus Came to Heal (Luke 4:18–19)

At the time the trumpet sounded at the fiftieth year, throughout the land, the people were free from debt and bondage. Families were united again. In that year of jubilee, God said there would be no labor; it would be a year of rest and peace.

Jesus declared that the jubilee was no longer a period of time but a person. He was saying, "I am the Jubilee of God. I am sent to bring deliverance to the captives. I will give you rest and peace."

You don't have to be blind anymore, sick anymore, poor anymore, or brokenhearted anymore.

Threefold Ministry of Jesus

> Jesus went about all Galilee, teaching in their synagogues and Preaching the gospel of the kingdom, and healing all manner of sickness and all manner of disease among the people. (Matthew 4:23)

His threefold ministry was teaching, preaching, and healing.

Jesus Healed All Who Came

> When the evening was come they brought unto HIM many that were possessed with devils and HE cast out

the spirits with HIS word and healed all that were sick. (Matthew 8:16)

And great multitudes followed HIM, and He healed them all. (Matthew 12:15)

And brought unto HIM all that were diseased; and as many as touched were made perfectly whole. (Matthew 14:35–36)

All they that had any sickness with divers diseases brought them unto HIM; and HE laid HIS hands on every one of them and healed them. (Luke 4:40)

He didn't pray for the sick; He healed them with a spoken word. Repeatedly throughout the Gospels, he healed them all. Most were healed immediately. He spoke as one with authority when praying for the sick. He told the devils, "Go!" He told blind eyes, "Open!" He told the dumb, "Speak!" He told the lame, "Pick up your bed and walk!" He told the dead, "Arise, wake up, and come forth!" He told the woman with an issue of blood, "Your faith has made you whole!"

Healing did not cease with Jesus; He left His healing power with us.

He that believeth on me, the works that I do shall he do also; and greater works than these shall he do; because I go to unto my father. (John 14:12)

If it were God's will for his people to be sick, why did He provide us these instructions?

They shall lay hands on the sick and they shall recover And these signs shall follow them who believe. In my name, they shall cast out devils, they shall speak with new tongues. They shall take up serpents and if they drink anything, it shall not hurt them. They shall lay hands on the sick and they shall recover. (Mark 16:17–18)

Call for the Elders of the Church

Is there any sick among you. Let him call for the elders of the church; and let them pray over him, anointing him with oil in the name of the lord: And the prayer of faith shall save the sick and the Lord shall raise him up. (James 5:14–16)

When a Believer Has the Special Gift of Healing

But the manifestation of the Spirit is given to every man to profit withal. To another the gifts of healing by the same Spirit; dividing to every man severally as He will. (1 Corinthians 12:7–9)

Fill Yourself with Promises from the Word of God

My son, attend to my words; incline thine ear unto my sayings. Let them not depart from thine eyes; keep them in the midst of thine heart. For they are life unto those that find them, and health to all their flesh. (Proverbs 4:20–23)

You Can Be Healed through a Spoken Word

Lord, I am not worthy that thou shouldest come under my roof. But speak the word only, and my servant shall be healed. (Matthew 8:8)

Facts about Divine Healing

It is God's will to heal you. Sickness doesn't come from God. There is more than one method by the Word of God to obtain healing. Healing is not always manifested instantly; sometimes, it comes gradually.

Some of Jesus's healings were not instant. The blind man wasn't healed immediately; he wasn't healed until he washed in the pool of

Siloam. There was a space of time between the time Jesus said "Go" and the time the man gained his sight (John 9:1–7).

Your Faith Will Make You Whole (Mark 5:27–30)

She heard (v. 27); faith comes by hearing. She said (v. 28); faith comes by confessing. She did something about it. Oral Roberts would say at times when he finished praying for someone, "Do something now that you could not do before."

Your Faith Is Important to Others

> And they come unto him, bringing one sick of the palsy, which was borne of four. And when they could not come nigh unto him for the press, they uncovered the roof where he was: and when they had broken it up, they let down the bed wherein the sick of the palsy lay. When Jesus saw their faith, he said unto the sick of the palsy, "Son, thy sins be forgiven thee." (Mark 2:3–5)

The scripture says that four men carried the cripple to the house where Jesus was. They cared about their paralyzed friend and brought him to see Jesus to be healed.

Prophecy

I am strength of my people. I was the strength of Israel, and I led them forth. I made the weak strong; I gave the old strength as the young. They marched victoriously. I gave them my strength. They walked through the Red Sea with my strength. The old as well as the young. I will give you my strength. Do not say it is not God's will for me to be delivered. Declare, "The Lord is my help, the Lord is my strength; I will not listen to what man says to me. He will not make my God weak in my eyes. He will not take the strength of my God from my heart. I refused to listen to anyone who will destroy my faith that God has given me."

I will lift you up and give you strength as I overshadow you. I have given you healing, but some of you won't use it. Some of you don't know how. I have sent my messenger with my power with my gifts, and yet when my servant touches you as my greatness goes in you, you cannot accept my healing. And you go from my house thinking, *Maybe I will get well,* and in that moment, you have turned your back on what I have promised you. And that is the reason so many of you are afflicted when you would be well. I have not been able to cure you because you won't let me. I could not have cured you of your sins had you doubted me and said, "Maybe my sins are gone," but you declare the Lord is my Savior.

Why not declare the Lord is my Healer? He has healed me! God has promised this, and God cannot lie.

God Heals the Wounded, the Bruised, and the Brokenhearted

Hurt is the number-one hijacker of dreams, purpose, life, joy, and destiny. It is the number-one way Satan uses to destroy people's lives, dreams, marriages, and relationships. Hurt is a destroyer of marriages, dreams, and destinies.

Hurt Hurts

Hurt is no respecter of persons. Hurt affects all people every day at work, at home, and even at church. I've seen and experienced many hurts and have asked, "God, where are you?"

Hurt Affects Us

Many people can be so mean; at times, church folk do not act like Jesus. I've learned you can be hurt more at church than anywhere else.

All your life, people have asked you how are you, and you said, "I'm fine. I'm doing well." You said all your life that things haven't affected you. But you're wrong, and if you want God to deal with it, He will do it right now. He can pull out the hurt you have suppressed for so long.

Hurt Forms Us

People pay hundreds to lie on a couch and hear what I'm giving you now. Hurt forms our behavior—how we act and even how we think.

Thousands of people have let their pasts form their identities. Their hurt and pain has formed how they think, talk, and behave. Your past and present hurt will try to tell you who you are. Hurt will try to label you and mark you as something and want you to live with that identity from hell for the rest of your life. That will affect everything socially.

Hurt People Hear Things Differently

When you are dealing with hurt, bitterness, and anger, you will hear things filtered through that. Somebody will say something to you, but you'll hear it in a totally different way because it is filtered through hurt.

You can even be offended by preachers thinking they're talking directly to you. But it's God trying to get through to you through your heart.

Hurt will cause you to hear through another set of ears. It will make you offended and even touchy.

Hurt People See Things Differently

You will have impaired vision; you will see things totally wrong. You will see false images about your boss, coworkers, neighbors, and those at church. Hurt can make you paranoid; it can make you think, "People are talking about me." You think you see something correctly, but hurt will distort the truth.

The enemy doesn't want anyone reading this to be free. Every day, some people quit church and ministry, saying, "I can't take it anymore. I can't take these folks anymore. That pastor really hurt me." They will make it sound like something else, but they're quitting because they hurt. Every day, people are quitting their marriages. They can't take it because they are hurt. And others are even quitting life.

Anybody ever hear of Jeremiah the prophet? He's called the weeping prophet. He's having a bad day; have you ever have a bad day?

> For since I spake, I cried out, I cried violence and spoil; because the word of the LORD was made a reproach unto me, and a derision, daily. Then I said, I will not make mention of him, nor speak any more in his name. (In

other words, I am done with church, I am quitting and I can't take it anymore) But his word was in mine heart as a burning fire shut up in my bones, and I was weary with forbearing, and I could not stay. (I wanted to quit but I can't, I still must do what God has called me to do) For I heard the defaming of many, fear on every side. (They're just waiting for me to fall). Report, say they, and we will report it. All my familiars watched for my halting, saying, peradventure he will be enticed, and we shall prevail against him, and we shall take our revenge on him. (Jeremiah 20:8–10)

Jeremiah is facing depression, rejection, bitterness, anger, and paranoia because he is hurting. That's what hurt will do to anybody. But it gets worse.

Cursed be the day wherein I was born: let not the day wherein my mother bears me be blessed. Cursed be the man who brought tidings to my father, saying, 'A man child is born unto thee'; making him very glad. And let that man be as the cities which the LORD overthrew, and repented not: and let him hear the cry in the morning, and the shouting at noontide; Because he slew me not from the womb; or that my mother might have been my grave, (My mother's womb been my grave) and her womb to be always great with me. Wherefore came I forth out of the womb to see labor and sorrow, that my days should be consumed with shame? (Jeremiah 20:14–18)

"I'm a mistake. I'm stupid. I can't do anything right. I wish God had never let me be born. I didn't want to be born to see this mess." Jeremiah is hurt to the point that he might take his own life.

The devil will tell you that your life is worthless, that nobody cares, that no one will notice if you're gone. But the devil is a liar; don't you dare touch your life.

We have to deal with hurt before we can experience new things with God. We said as kids, "Sticks and stones may break my bones but names will never hurt me." There has never been a statement more wrong than that. Words *will* hurt you—things people have spoken over you or said about you. Words will hurt you—names your dad called you, things your ex keeps saying about you.

Four Things Concerning Hurt—

1. Stop Cursing It

We're always tempted to get even with others who have hurt us, to take the situation into our own hands because of hurts we've suffered at the hands of others. We think, *I want them to pay.* The enemy wants you to get even, but that's sin. And the moment you get into sin, God can't move on your behalf. Don't let it become a root of bitterness. The Bible says, "Casting all your cares upon him for He careth for you."

> Do not deliver me to the will of my adversaries; For false witnesses have risen against me, and such as breathe out violence. I would have lost heart, unless I had believed that I would see the goodness of the Lord in the land of the living. (Psalm 27:12–13 NKJV)

That means, "I would have lost my mind; I have really been hurt." It's tough when people hurt you, but it's even worse when it's people close to you.

2. Stop Rehearsing It

This is big. There comes a time when you have to stop rehashing the past. Quit playing the DVD of what happened to you. Quit playing it every Friday night and eating candy and popcorn. It's a trap of the enemy to get you to stay in this land and not get to the land of promise. Stop playing it and rehashing it in your head. Stop saying, "If only I had not done ..." That will keep you from going forward, and it will never change your past.

As long as you're rehashing your past, you can't cry out to God, "God, I want you to move in my life!" God can't move until you do. If you have anything against anyone, forgive him. Leave it. Let it go so your Father will forgive you your failings and shortcomings and let them drop. Get rid of the unforgiveness in your heart.

If the Bible says that God will not hear our prayers because of unforgiveness, what makes us think the devil will hear our rebuke? (Mark 11:25 NKJV)

3. Stop Nursing It

Decide to move on; don't build your house in the land of pain. Don't sit for twenty years on this side of the Jordan. Decide to be healed; otherwise, grief will hang out with you forever.

Deuteronomy 34:8 says something powerful about grieving. Moses has just died, and everybody is grieving; they are hurt. God shows up and says, "I am giving you thirty days to grieve and then at that point stop."

You ask, "God, why are you being so insensitive? I just had a death in my family. Only thirty days to grieve?" God puts a statute of limitations on our grief and hurt. God says, "I'll let you deal with it for thirty days to pray it out. After that, get up from beside Moses's grave and move into the Promised Land."

It's time for you to get up and be healed; God has so much more for you. Move out of the house of pain and move into the land of promise. You have been living in a prison of hurt and pain and then you fake it at church.

4. Reverse It

Turn the tables on the enemy. Use for good what the devil meant for evil. Decide to stop moping and digging things out of your past. Quit licking your wounds.

Remember when we were kids and would scrape our knees? A scab would form, and we'd scratch it, and our mothers would say, "Stop scratching it! Let it heal. Leave it alone!"

You know when you're being healed when you can say, "It is good for me that I have been afflicted, that I might learn Your statutes" (Psalm

119:71 NKJV). You say, "It's all right. I've been through some stuff, but I'm not the same person I was two years ago because I chose God's way. I don't harbor unforgiveness; I don't want to get even by poking holes in his tires. No, I decided to give God my pain, my hurt; I exchanged my sorrows for His joy. It's good that I went through all that stuff. Because I got hold of Jesus. I have His Word in my heart."

> Do not remember the former things, nor consider the things of old. Behold, I will do a new thing. Now it shall spring forth; shall you not know it? I will even make a road in the wilderness and rivers in the desert. (Isaiah 43:18–19 NKJV)

4. Jehovah Shalom—The Lord Is Peace

> Then Gideon built an altar there unto the Lord, and
> called it Jehovah Shalom—THE LORD IS PEACE.
> (Judges 6:24)

These verses tell us how the Midianites were destroying the fields and villages of the Israelites. The Midianites wanted to drive them out of Canaan. What's making life miserable for you?

The Israelites were worried about their enemies. But God said, "Don't you remember how I brought you out of Egypt? Don't you remember the victories I gave you when you first entered the land? You're in this mess because you forgot my promises. You're afraid because you've forgotten how powerful I am."

God brings peace to Israel through Gideon. With some trumpets, Gideon and his 300 men sent the Midianites fleeing for home without fighting at all.

The Bible records the country was in quietness forty years in the days of Gideon. If God brought peace to a nation, He can bring peace to a person. The Lord is peace; when problems come, He will be our peace.

The World's Attempt at Worldwide Peace

Today, peace is universally sought and talked about. We see diplomats all over the globe trying to obtain peace. The United Nations was established to ensure worldwide peace. We have summit conferences. Every four years, we have the Olympics at which nations get together to foster peace. But there will be no world peace until the Prince of Peace comes.

> When Jesus comes back, then weapons will be beaten
> into plowshares, and their spears into pruning hooks:
> and nations will no longer rise against nation, neither
> shall they learn war anymore. (Isaiah 2:4)

Mankind will then live in harmony. The wolf and the lamb shall feed together, and the lion shall eat straw like the bullock. They will not hurt nor destroy in all my holy mountain, saith the Lord. (Isaiah 65:25)

Individual Peace

People are constantly looking for peace; hundreds of people die every year not from overwork but from over worry. Our problem is not what we eat but what's eating us.

For some, recreation is the answer. For others, a vacation is the answer. If I could work only one week a year and have the other fifty-two weeks off, I'd be happy.

Others have mistaken alcohol and drugs for peace, but they find out that after they come back down or up, they still have the same problems and more. None of these can bring peace. Because there is no peace, we have so many suicides and divorces.

For God has not given us the spirit of fear. (2 Timothy 1:7)

Fear is the opposite of peace.

There is no fear in love; but perfect love casteth out fear: because fear hath torment. He that feareth is not made perfect in love. (1 John 4:18)

But the wicked are like the troubled sea, when it cannot rest, whose waters cast up mire and dirt. There is no peace saith my God to the wicked. (Isaiah 57:20–21)

Without God, we will never be at peace with ourselves or others. To be at peace with ourselves and others requires Jesus Christ.

And having made peace through the blood of His cross, by Him to reconcile all things unto Himself. (Colossians 1:20)

> Therefore being justified by faith, we have peace with
> God through our Lord Jesus Christ. (Romans 5:1)

> There is therefore now no condemnation to them which
> are in Christ Jesus, who walk not after the flesh, but after
> the spirit. (Romans 8:1)

The Peace of God

Those who have made peace with God have the peace of God. Being born again gives us the peace of God. Sadly, many Christians have made peace *with* God but do not have the peace *of* God. We have Christians who have known God for a long time but do not have the peace of God. Are they going to heaven? Yes. Do they love the Lord? Yes.

> Peace I leave with you, my peace I give unto you, not as
> the world giveth, give I unto you. Let not your heart be
> trouble. (John 14:27)

The peace of the world says, "If my bank account has this much money in it ..." Jesus said, though, that the peace He gives us comes from God.

David knew that peace even when he was being hunted like an animal and sleeping in caves. Saul was out to kill him. In the midst of all of this, he wrote, "I will both lay me down in peace, and sleep: For thou, Lord, only makest me dwell in safety" (Psalm 4:8).

Stephen knew that peace in Acts 7:54–60. How can a person be at peace while under attack? They were stoning him, but his face shone like an angel's. We can be at peace too even when we're being attacked physically or spiritually.

Peter knew that peace. In Acts 12:1–11, Peter was to be executed the next day. The angel of the Lord came to him and found him asleep between two guards. How many of us would get a good night's sleep if you knew your head was going to be cut off the next day? The angel had to hit him to wake him up.

The apostle Paul knew that peace. In Acts 27:21–44, he was on a ship in a terrible storm for a number of days. It was so bad that the sailors had thrown everything they could overboard. Their ship was coming apart. Paul told them, "Be of good cheer." The others calmed down when they saw the peace of God all over him.

> Thou will keep him in perfect peace, whose mind is stayed on thee: Because he trusteth un thee. (Isaiah 26:3)

If you don't have perfect peace, it's because your mind is in the wrong place; it's not fixed on Him.

The Peace of God Does Not Come Automatically

> Be careful for nothing (means don't worry). But in everything by prayer and supplication with thanksgiving let your request be made known unto God. AND THE PEACE OF GOD, WHICH PASSETH ALL UNDERSTANDING, SHALL KEEP YOUR HEARTS AND MINDS THROUGH JESUS CHRIST. Finally, brethren, whatsoever things are TRUE, whatsoever things are JUST, whatsoever things are PURE, whatsoever things are LOVELY, whatsoever things are of a GOOD REPORT, think on these things. Those things that you have both learned, and received, and heard, and seen in me, do: and THE GOD OF PEACE SHALL BE WITH YOU. (Philippians 4:6–9)

I meditate on that which is pure, true, just, lovely and of a good report. Not the six o'clock news, not CNN, and not Fox News.

Cast Your Cares on Him

> Casting all your cares upon Him, for He careth for you. (1 Peter 5:7)

Once and for all, cast all your anxieties, worries, concerns, on Him because He cares for you affectionately and cares about you watchfully. Give all your burdens to God; don't ask Him to lighten your load; they will no longer be yours but His. Taking pills so you're not up all night is evidence that you're not handling your cares that well.

We want God to take care of our problems, but every time God reaches for them, we put our hands back on them; we don't turn them loose. God cannot take them if we don't let go of them. How many of us are truly carefree?

True Story

The driver of a flatbed truck saw someone carrying a big, heavy load on his back and was hardly making it he was so bent over. The driver pulled over and said, "Let me give you a ride." The man said, "I don't want to put you out any. I'll just get on back and ride."

They went a little way, and the driver looked into his mirror and saw this guy sitting with his backpack still on his back. He pulled over, went to the back of the truck, and asked, "Why don't you set that thing down?" The man replied, "It's enough that you're carrying me. I won't ask you to carry my load too."

We're like that. We say, "God, help me and carry me." "How about that load?" He asks. We say, "Oh God, I couldn't ask you to take that on too." We lay it on the altar but then pick it back up and walk out with it.

> Come unto me, all ye labor, and are heavy laden and I will give you rest. Take my yoke upon you and learn of me: For I am meek and lowly in heart: And you shall find rest unto your souls. (Matthew 11:28–29)

Worry Nullifies Prayer

> Be careful for nothing; but in everything by prayer and supplication with thanksgiving let your request be made known unto God. (Philippians 4:6)

As long as you fret and have anxiety about what you're praying about, you're nullifying the effects of your praying. You haven't cast it on the Lord; you still have it. In this life, you'll never be exempt from problems. I say that not to depress you but so you won't be walking around in a daze thinking that when you made Jesus Lord of your life, everything was going to be all right.

> When affliction or persecution ariseth (not if). (Mark 4:17)

Jesus said that we would have tribulation in this world.

> Many are the affliction of the righteous (They will come). But the Word of God does not stop there: "But the Lord delivers them from them all." (Psalm 34:19)

Peace is not the absence of problems but the peace of God that passes all understanding. Satan wants to take from us the peace God gives us. The Bible says in the last days, men's hearts will fail them for fear as they look at the things coming upon the earth.

Grace and Peace

> Grace be unto you, and peace, from God our Father. (Ephesians 1:2)

Grace always comes before peace. Before you can have peace in your life, you have to understand the grace of God. Once you understand grace, you will begin to understand peace and understand God has already done all the work.

Ephesians 2:8 tells us, "For by Grace are ye saved through faith; and that not of yourselves: it is the gift of God, not of works, least any man should boast." Trying to work to please God? Nothing pleases God but faith in the finished work of Jesus Christ on the cross.

Grace and Peace Can Be Multiplied

> Grace and peace be multiplied unto you through the knowledge of God, and of Jesus our Lord. (2 Peter 1:2)

Understanding of God's Word, always increases more of His blessings in our life.

5. Jehovah Shammah—The Lord Is Present

> It was round about eighteen thousand measures: and
> the name of the city from that day shall be called THE
> LORD IS THERE. (Ezekiel 48:35)

God revealed that this would be the name of the Holy City, the New Jerusalem—Jehovah Shammah, the Lord is there. The name reveals that God chooses to live among humanity. "Whenever there are two or three gathered in my name, I am in the midst of them. He is the one in the midst of two or three. Doesn't it say, "God inhabits the praises of his people"?

The word *inhabits* is an interesting word in Hebrew; it means "enthrone." It means when you praise Him, you offer up to God a throne, He sits on the throne, gives executive orders and directions, and directs principalities to go in directions they do not want to go. He commands them to go simply because you have given God a throne by your praise.

God has made us kings and priests with authority and spiritual access. In the Old Testament, the priest offered sacrifices; in the New Testament, the priest offers sacrifices of praise and worship to the Father.

The major responsibly of a saint is giving God praise. Psalm 102 speaks about praise. A prophecy is given about the future of Israel and your life till the coming of the Messiah. Then five prophecies are mentioned.

1. God will arise.
2. Have mercy on Zion.
3. A time to favor her.
4. The heathen shall fear the name of the Lord.
5. The Lord will build up Zion.

This prophecy was written for the generation to come. God is looking for one thing concerning the definition of the last generation that will see the coming of the Messiah and a manifestation of power the body of Christ has never seen before. This generation will know how to praise Him. A priest is authorized to offer sacrifices of praise to the Lord.

Only the priest shall bear the ark. The priest has the power of praise. The priest has the authority to speak to the Father. The priest shall go before the ark because the presence of God will follow the cloud and follow the praise. The presence of God will never follow your depression, your fear, your lust, your bondage, or anything that pertains to the flesh. The presence of God will follow only the priest who zeroes in on the praise, worship, and honor of the King of Kings and the Lord of Lords.

The ark in the Hebrew means the chest of God or the heart of God; the heart of God follows the priest with the praise. The ark was the throne of God on earth. Whenever the children of Israel had the ark in their possession, no enemy could overcome them because the ark represented the heart and throne of God.

As a priest who praises God and magnifies and glorifies His name, you will have the throne of God, the chest of God, and the authority of God with you.

The greatest attack on the body of Christ, the greatest attack on Christians has been the attack on your praise that is meant to redirect your worship. The enemy knows that if he can distract your worship, he can distract you from your tour of duty. The enemy can take your praise and put it somewhere where there is no presence, no power, no throne.

Take your praise back, take your worship back, take the spiritual function you were destined for back. Let your enemies know that your body was created to be a temple of God, your lips were created to express praise, your spirit was created to worship God in heaven and here on earth.

Let the enemy know you will not be robbed of the prime responsibility God has given you to be a spiritual connection through your praise and worship. The priest has to go before the ark to lead people. If people have to be led, if people are to follow, let them follow the worshiper. If people have to follow you, let them not follow your reputation, let them not follow your accomplishments, let them not follow all the things you have done in your life, your gifts and everything that brings applause in your life. If people are to follow you, if they are going to go where they can pull down strongholds, let them be people who follow your praise.

Church, It's Time to Sing

> By the rivers of Babylon, there we sat down, yea, we wept
> when we remembered Zion. We hung our harps upon the
> willows in the midst of it. For those who carried us away
> captive required of us a song. And those who plundered
> us required of us mirth, Saying, sing us of the songs of
> Zion! HOW SHALL WE SING THE LORD'S SONG
> IN A STRANGE LAND. (Psalm 137:1–4)

The Babylonian Empire had taken the Israelites captive and took
them to a land they knew not; it was a place of rivers, streams, and willow
trees. The Bible says that when they got to this area, they sat and wept as
they remembered Zion, symbolic of the church and the glory of the Lord.
They remembered Zion, they remembered the presence of the Lord, and
they remembered the *shekinah* glory of God.

They Sat in the Willow Trees

They sat. They had lost their strength. They could no longer go on.
Have you ever lost your strength? When you couldn't even put one foot
in front of the other? Has discouragement weighed on you so heavily that
you didn't know which way to go? Has disease, sickness, and oppression
come upon you to the point that you didn't know which way to turn?
That's where the children of Israel were.

The Enemy's Request

Their enemy told them, "Come on and sing if you can. You once beat
your tambourines and played your instruments as you sang before the
Lord. Let's see you sing now. Let's hear you produce a beautiful note now."
They did it mockingly—"Can you sing now?"

I say, church, that's the time to break out in song! Send up a sacrifice of
singing. That's the time to let the devil know there's nothing too difficult
for the Lord.

When is it time to sing?

In the darkest hour, it's time to sing.

In the valley of valleys, it's time to sing.
In the midst of the storm, it's time to sing.
When the enemy mocks you, it's time to sing.
When friends fail you, it's time to sing.
When you've lost a loved one, it's time to sing.
When you lose your job, it's time to sing.
When you don't know which way to turn, it's time to sing.
When cancer enters your body, it's time to sing.

We're Living in a Day

We're living in a day that if my home gets blessed, or if I get that car I want, or if I get that raise, I'll start singing. We're living in a day that if everything is going our way and everything is being handed to us on a silver platter, we can sing all kinds of songs. We're living in a day that when we begin to sing, people will flop down in their chairs and not get involved in the singing and worshiping. We're living in a day that everybody is making excuses. The devil doesn't have to knock you down anymore.

One guy walked out of the church and saw a devil sitting and crying. He asked the devil, "What's wrong?" The devil said, "They're blaming me for things I've never done."

If the devil had the power that some of you think he does, you'd never have made it to church today. So why come to church just to sit? Why come to church just to act defeated?

I am glad I can sing if the bottom falls out. I can sing in the darkest hour. I can sing when the devil thinks he's got me. Listen to me—don't lose your song no matter what happens.

We Will All Be Tested

I'm not talking about things such as people aggravating you on the job. I'm not talking about everyday life. I'm talking about when the devil looks down his double-barreled shotgun and says, "Those are the souls I want, and I'll do everything I can to put the pressure on them until I see them squirm like worms."

I'm talking about when the devil unleashes the hordes of hell and they come out of the bottomless pit with fire breathing out of their mouths ready to devour you. Can you look up then and sing the songs of Zion? Can you shout when everything is falling all around you? Can you praise the Lord? God says you can. God says, "Sing on, church. Don't hang your harps up. Keep on singing."

Some People Remind Me of Statues

Water is flowing out of their mouths, but they haven't ever tasted one drop of it. We have people singing songs, but they don't know what they're singing about. We have people preaching, but they don't know what they're preaching about.

You can be like that statue, or you can be like that child of God out of whom rivers of living water flow. If the world can excite you and heaven can't, there's something wrong with your exciter. If the glory of God doesn't excite you, you need to find out what's keeping you from rejoicing.

What Is Your Real Goal?

If the goal of Zion would have been to praise God no matter what the situation was, the harps would not have been hanging in the willow trees; they would have been being played.

It's time for us to get rid of our pacifiers and milk bottles and start standing on our own two feet for the Lord. I know why some of you can't shout; it's because you're not living right. If you fall in love with Jesus again, you'll get a song in your heart again.

You Have to Sing

If you want something from the Lord, you can't just say, "Drop it down on me, Lord." Blessed are they who hunger and thirst for righteousness; they shall be filled. I am hungry. I want to sing. How many of you have a song? Where's your harp? Have you sung your favorite song lately, or is your harp hanging in the willow trees? Do you want to drive the devil out of your life? The oppression out of your life? You have to sing.

What did the man do when Paul and Silas said, "Silver and gold I have none"? He got up. He leaped. Have you lost your leap? He went away walking, leaping, and praising God.

Have you lost your song? Where's your harp? Are you in prison? Has the devil locked you up? Has sin bound you to the point that you can't get free? Get a song. It's time to sing. I want to see the Lord deliver you and put a song in your heart. Lord, I refuse to let the enemy take my song. He won't take it. I'm going to sing the songs of Zion.

If you're bound, God wants to set you free. You know you're bound, the devil knows you're bound, and God knows you're bound, but you're trying to cover it up and act as if nothing's wrong. But you're bound in your heart. You feel the chain as it pulls tight against your very soul. Brother and sister, there's a chain breaker here, someone who will liberate you from the devil's strongholds in your life.

6. Jehovah Tsidkenu—The Lord Our Righteousness

> Behold, the days come saith the Lord, that I will raise unto David a righteous branch, and a king shall reign and prosper, and shall execute judgment and justice in the earth. In his days Judah shall be saved, and Israel shall dwell safely: and this is his name whereby he shall be called, "THE LORD OUR RIGHTEOUSNESS!" (Jeremiah 23:5–6)

The Lord our righteousness! One day, the earth will rejoice in His righteousness. Any righteousness a child of God has is merely the imputed righteousness of Christ.

> And therefore it was imputed to him for righteousness. Now it was not written for his sake only, but it was imputed to him; but for us also, to whom it shall be imputed, if we believe on Him that raised up Jesus our Lord from the dead; Who was delivered for our offences, and was raised again for our justification. (Romans 4:22–25, about Abraham)

God Wants to Give Us the Holiness We Can Never Achieve on Our Own

When we enter heaven, we aren't going to say we made it there because of our own good deeds. Isaiah 64:6 reads, "But we are all as an unclean thing, and all our righteousness are as filthy rags; and we all do fade as a leaf; and our iniquities, like the wind, have taken us away." We will say, "The Lord is our righteousness. He has made everything right with God the Father."

Jesus has become our righteousness; when we receive Him, we become as righteous as He is in our heavenly Father's sight. We put on His robe of righteousness. The Word of God tells us that when the Living God looks at us, He sees us just as pure as He sees Jesus even when we're not behaving so righteously.

"I am the righteousness of God." We should say that several times a day to remind ourselves of this.

7. Jehovah Rohi—The Lord Is My Shepherd

Psalm 23 is probably the best-known passage of scripture. All seven of the redemptive names of Jehovah can be found in the Psalms: "The Lord is my shepherd I shall not want." (Jehovah Rohi and Jireh)

Sheep have been referred to as the dumbest animals ever, but the Lord said, "I will be a shepherd to you." He's the Good Shepherd who provides for His sheep. He knows them. He leads them. He talks to them. He searches for them. He delivers them from their enemies. He gives them rest in green pastures. He heals them. He would die for them.

David said, "My shepherd gives me the best, so I shall boldly say I shall not want."

> For the Lord thy God hath blessed thee in all the works of thy hand: he knoweth thy walking through this great wilderness these forty years the Lord thy God hath been with thee; thou hast lacked nothing. (Deuteronomy 2:7)

He leadeth me beside the still waters. (Jehovah Shalom)

God does not lead His people to standing water that gathers filth, nor to rapid floods, but to silent, pure water. Still water is easy to reach and drink.

> Whosoever drinketh of this water will thirst again: but whosoever drinketh of the water that I shall give him will never thirst. But the water that I shall give him shall be in him a well of water springing up into everlasting life. (John 4:13–14)

He restoreth my soul. (Jehovah Ralph)

Restore and *renew* have the same meaning. "But they that wait upon the Lord shall renew their strength, they shall mount up as wings of eagles" (Isaiah 40:31).

As young eagles grow, they lose their strong pinion feathers. But as they grow older, they grow new and stronger feathers. Older eagles can fly higher that they did when they were younger; they are stronger than they were when they were younger.

He leadeth me in the paths of righteousness for his name sake. (Jehovah Tiskenu)

Jehovah is Himself perfect righteousness. A God of truth and without iniquity, just and right is He.

Man has no righteousness: "As it is written, there is none righteous, no, not one" (Romans 3:10). "But we are all as an unclean thing, and all our righteousness's are as filthy rags; and we all do fade as a leaf; and our iniquities, like the wind, have taken us away" (Isaiah 64:6). The Bible makes it clear that righteousness is impossible to be attained by man alone: "Behold, I was shapen in iniquity; and in sin did my mother conceive me" (Psalm 51:5). "How then can man be justified with God? Or how can he be clean that is born of a woman?" (Job 25:4).

Since we are unrighteous, we need pardon from God.

> I will greatly rejoice in the LORD, my soul shall be joyful in my God; for he hath clothed me with the garments of salvation, he hath covered me with the robe of righteousness, as a bridegroom decketh himself with ornaments, and as a bride adorneth herself with her jewels. (Isaiah 61:10)

Yea, though I walk thought the valley of the shadow of death, I will fear no evil. (Jehovah Shammah)

The valley of the shadow of death was a real place. No shepherd would take his sheep there unless he had to because it was too dangerous. Steep cliffs, wild beasts. The sheep needed water so badly that the shepherd had to take them through the valley because only there could water be found.

But David said going through it, we don't have to fear evil. Not because there is none but because our Shepherd is with us and will not take his eyes off us. I will fear no evil though I walk through it. We need not fear evil. Death cannot separate us from the love of God.

Storms That Come against Us (Mark 4:35–41)

The Sea of Galilee is about fourteen miles long and eight miles wide. In just a few minutes, a storm could arise and destroy ships. So many would be lost when storms came; they were at the mercy of the sea, which showed none.

The disciples knew these things. Jesus said, "Let us go over to the other side." Jesus and His disciples launched into the sea that evening, and a storm arose that battered the ship as if it were a toy. They did everything that experienced sailors knew to do. Perhaps they lowered the sail and dumped cargo to make the ship lighter. They had done everything they could, but it didn't seem to be enough.

Some of us have done everything humanly possible to come out of storms that have battered us and ended up thinking we didn't stand a chance.

Somebody remembered Jesus was onboard: "For thou art with me." Jesus had not bailed out when the storm hit; even when it looked like the boat was going down, He stayed onboard with them.

Beloved, if you have asked Jesus to come onboard in your life, I assure you He is still onboard. He hasn't forsaken you in your time of great need.

The disciples saw that He was sleeping, and they were upset. Jesus was experiencing the same storm they were but was sleeping through it.

Storm may be raging in your life, but Jesus wants you to be at peace. Psalm 4:8 reads, "I will both lay me down in peace, and sleep: For thou, Lord, only makes me dwell in safety."

The disciples awakened Him and asked, "Lord, don't you care we're about to perish?" Jesus looked into the eye of that storm and said, "Peace. Be still." Then there was a great calm. The storm was gone. The disciples made it to the other side.

You are not just a person; you are the temple of the Living God, and He said, "I will live in them and walk with them and dwell in them."

They had the Lord with them, but we have him in us. Is God sending these storms against us? Why are these things happening to us? Realize that God does not send storms. God did not send that storm on the Sea of Galilee. If God had done this, we would have a breaking of the Word of God. Jesus said, "I and my Father are one." If Jesus had rebuked the storm, He would have been rebuking the Father.

God is not sending the storm in your life. Why is your boat being rocked? Because the devil wants you to doubt. He wants you to believe you're going to drown. He does not want you to believe you can make it, so he roars out against you with a storm. He doesn't believe you have the faith to go over, and you won't trust God to get you out of it. He thinks he will capsize your boat. But remember that Jesus is onboard in good times and bad. The good news is that all our storms will come to an end.

In Acts 27:30–31, Paul told everyone to stay on the ship because it was safer there because Jesus was onboard. We are not exempt from storms; Jesus said, "In this world, you will have tribulation." But if you jump ship, you'll never make it. Remember—Jesus is onboard.

Contrary Winds, Spiritual Powers at Work

> And when we had launched from thence, we sailed under
> Cyprus, because the winds were contrary. (Acts 27:4)

Winds are important in the Bible literally and figuratively. The four winds are limits of distances or direction. Of the cardinal directions, the east wind is most frequently mentioned. It is stormy, it wrecks ships, and it withers growing things. The north wind brings rain and is refreshing. The south wind is gentle and fosters growth. The west wind blew away the plague of locusts. Winds blow chaff away, fulfill God's command, reveal weakness and worthlessness, and clear the sky. God rides on the wings of wind, which has a drying effect. Winds can be helpful; they push sailboats along.

But I want to talk about contrary winds—spiritual powers that work against us. Believers are warned about the evil winds of false doctrine.

> Therefore whoever hears these sayings of mine, and does
> them. I will liken him to a wiser man who built his house
> on the Rock: And the rain descended, the floods came,
> and the winds blew and beat on that house; and it did not

fall because it was founded upon a rock. Now everyone who hears these sayings of mine, and does not do them, will be like a foolish man who built his house on sand: And the rain descended, the floods came, and the winds blew and beat on that house; and it fell. And great was its fall. (Matthew 7:24–27)

We're living in difficult times, very pressing times, times that will squash the very life out of us. But He is still able to help us if only we look to Him.

Many Christians are not in the victory lane; they are constantly being battered, and there is no victory in sight. I want to tell them that God intends for them to live victorious lives.

Obedience

Then Samuel said: Has the Lord great delight in burnt offerings and sacrifices, as in obeying the voice of the Lord? Behold, to obey is better than sacrifice, and to heed than the fat of rams. For rebellion is as the sin of witchcraft, and stubbornness is as iniquity and idolatry. Because you have rejected the Word of the Lord, He has rejected you from being king. (1 Samuel 15:22–23)

Obedience is where the solid foundations begins. You can sing well, you can teach, you can preach, you can do all kinds of things. But if you aren't obedient to the Word of God, you will face difficult times without anything to stand on.

Disobedience is why a lot of us are in trouble. God is able to help us in difficult times, but we must be obedient at all times. Obedience will give us strength in times of trials. If we've been obedient to the Lord, tried to please the Lord, and lived the best we could, we won't have to hang our heads to talk with God when difficult times come.

A man went to build a house. The scripture calls him a wise man because he built on a rock, a solid foundation.

> For in the time of trouble he shall hide me in His pavilion:
> In the secret of His tabernacle shall He hide me; He shall
> set me upon a Rock. (Psalm 27:50)

When you get in a difficult situation, you should not sit there and ask, "Why did this happen to me?" You should rejoice. In obedience, in the most difficult and trying times, you need to praise the Lord. There is strength in obedience and in praising the Lord, lifting your head and hands, looking up to the Lord, and trusting in Him during hard times.

Obedience is the foundation of victorious Christian living. Through obedience, you will find your feet planted on a solid, unmovable, unshakeable foundation. I have trusted in Jesus and found Him to be that rock that will hold you up in the most difficult times. When it feels like you don't know which way to turn. When there are dark clouds of oppression on every side. When evil would harm you. When temptation would drag you down.

If you want the key to victorious living, do what the Lord tells you. It may sound too simple, but if you obey the Lord, you will be able to withstand the storms of life. When you are obedient to the Word, you can stand in the face of temptations and trials and say, "No, devil, no, world, I'm not going to follow you. I'm going to follow Jesus Christ."

Rain

Rain can be good or destructive. Enough rain can make your crops grow; too much rain can make them rot. You can look afar and see the clouds gathering and you can say, "It's going to rain." Then there are those that move in unexpectedly and bring in a great downpour.

Floods

Floods sometimes come after the rain. Notice the floods came against this house. This is overwhelming. Have you ever been overwhelmed? Have you ever been to a point that you didn't know which way to turn? I know what it's like to feel the floods come in. There's nobody to turn to; you don't have any friends in the world. You don't know whom to call.

You're overwhelmed. Everything is out of proportion. That's what he was saying about this house.

Someday, you will be tested by something overwhelming with such force that if you're not on a solid foundation, your house will cave in. But thank God that Jesus Christ is that tried-and-true foundation who will hold your house up during trials and trying times.

Wind

In this case, it wasn't a gentle breeze that moves leaves around. It was a destructive wind that meant business—first-degree murder was out to destroy this house. Rain, flood, wind—you tried your best, but in the face of all opposition, I'm still standing.

Easy Prey for the Devil

The key again is obedience. It doesn't matter how many times you go to church—if you're not obedient to the Lord Jesus Christ, you're prey for the devil. If you're not founded on Jesus Christ, you're prey for the devil.

People live on certain scriptures; that's all they know. But obedience is where it's at. Obedience is victory. You know you have obeyed God, so nothing can move you; you can take whatever comes your way. There are storms in your life, and you're nervous when they come and happy when they go. The song says, "When the long night has ended and the storms come no more, let me stand in thy presence on that bright, peaceful shore." In the land where the tempest never comes, Lord, keep me safe until the storm passes by.

There are some right now in the midst of storms who need help. God wants to bring them help in contrary winds, things that are mounting against them. It may be sin; it may be disobedience to the Lord.

Didn't it make you feel good when you did something your parents asked you to do? You stood tall. You knew that the job had been done right, and you didn't hide your head. But if you did it just half right or didn't do it at all, how did you feel?

There are hearts right now God is speaking to. There are storms in your life, and God wants to help you now.

Thou preparest a table before me in the presence of mine enemies. (Jehovah Nissi— Lord our Banner/Our Conquer).

He says He will set a table for us in front of our enemies. The word for *table* in this verse means "spread." He's talking about a massive feast for only one person—you. God declares that this feast is a time for laughter, joy, and singing. He tells you, "Eat, drink, rejoice, and be glad." Your enemies are in shock. They're forced to observe how the Lord serves you. Jesus tells us that the Father does this for all His children.

> Blessed are those servants, whom the Lord when he cometh shall find watching: verily I say unto you, that he shall gird himself, and make them to sit down to meat, and will come forth and serve them. (Luke 12:37)

Thou anointest my head with oil. (Jehovah Mgaddisheem Sanctifies)

You anoint the head of someone who is being set aside for service. God anoints the heads of all His sheep because He has a job for them. As the oil flows from the crown of the head to the souls of the feet, it touches the head—the mind of Christ, the eyes—seeing as Christ sees, the mouth—our words, the ears—to hear the Spirit, the shoulders—to bear responsibility, the hands—to build and heal, the heart—salvation, and the feet—to take the good news to our neighbors.

My Cup Runneth Over

He will open the storehouse windows and pour us out a blessing if we obey Him. But if there is unconfessed sin in our lives, our lives can't run over.

> And it shall come to pass, if thou shall hearken diligently unto the voice of the Lord thy God, to observe and to do all his commandments which I command thee this day, that the Lord thy God will set thee high above all nations

of the earth: And all these blessings shall come on thee, and overtake thee, if thou will hearken unto the voice of the Lord thy God. Blessed shalt thou be when thou comest in, blessed shall thou be when thou goest out. The Lord shall cause thine enemies that rise up against you to be smitten, they shall come out against thee one way and flee before thee seven ways. The Lord shall command the blessings upon thee in thy store houses, and all that thou settest thine hand unto. And all the people of the earth shall see thou art called by the name of the Lord, and they shall be afraid of thee. The Lord shall open unto thee His good treasures, the heaven to give the rain unto thy land in his season, and to bless all thy work of thine hand: and thou shall lend unto many nations and not borrow. And the Lord shall make thee the head and not the tail; and thou shall be above only, and thou shall not be beneath. (Deuteronomy 28:1–13)

"Surely goodness and mercy shall follow me all the days of my life": mercy will blot out my sins while His goodness supplies all my needs. The Shepherd leads me, and His mercy and goodness follow me.

"And I will dwell in the house of the Lord forever": the mansion Jesus has built for us, His permanent guests.

"Let not your heart be troubled; believe in God, believe also in me. In my Father's house are many mansions" (John 14:1–3): Jesus the carpenter is building a mansion just for you.

David said, "The Lord is my Shepherd and I shall not lack." When his soul needed refreshment, the Shepherd provided him with green pastures. When his soul was weary, the Shepherd gave him still waters. When his soul needed revival, the Shepherd restored him. When his soul needed guidance, the Shepherd led him in paths of righteousness. When his soul was confronted with death, the Shepherd was with him. When his soul was confronted with enemies, the Shepherd provided his victory table. When his soul was wounded, the Shepherd poured in oil and wine. When his soul needed companionship, the Shepherd gave him goodness and mercy to follow him. And when David would leave this temporary earthly dwelling place, the Shepherd would provide a permanent heavenly dwelling place.

II. The Covenant Names of Jehovah

8. Jehovah-'Ez-Lami and Jehovah-Chezeq—Lord, My Strength

Here are three verses where "Lord my strength" appears.

> The LORD is my strength and song, and he is become my salvation: he is my God, and I will prepare him a habitation; my father's God, and I will exalt him. (Exodus 15:2)

> The LORD is my strength and my shield; my heart trusted in him, and I am helped: therefore my heart greatly rejoiceth; and with my song will I praise him. (Psalm 28:7)

> A Psalm of David, the servant of the LORD, who spake unto the LORD the words of this song in the day that the LORD delivered him from the hand of all his enemies, and from the hand of Saul: And he said, "I will love thee,

O LORD, my strength. The LORD is my rock, and my
fortress, and my deliverer; my God, my strength, in whom
I will trust; my buckler, and the horn of my salvation, and
my high tower. I will call upon the LORD, who is worthy
to be praised: so, shall I be saved from mine enemies."
(Psalm 18:1–3)

The first verse speaks about the song of Moses. In Exodus 15, the Lord
rescued the Hebrew people from Pharaohs' army.

In Psalm 18, David was celebrating God's hearing his prayer. These
verses are times of crying out to God in time of need and God's answers.
Moses said, "The Lord is my strength and song." David said, "The Lord is
my strength and my shield." Moses and David called God their strength.
Moses said He was a song, and David called Him a shield.

Fear and depression are defeated by worship and praise of God, who
will shield us from them.

David and Goliath

The Philistines stood on a mountain on one side, and
Israel stood on a mountain on the other side, with a
valley between them. And a champion went out from
the camp of the Philistines, named Goliath, from Gath,
whose height was six cubits and a span. He had a bronze
helmet on his head, and he was armed with a coat of
mail, and the weight of the coat was five thousand shekels
of bronze. And he had bronze armor on his legs and a
bronze javelin between his shoulders. Now the staff of
his spear was like a weaver's beam, and his iron spearhead
weighed six hundred shekels; and a shield-bearer went
before him. Then he stood and cried out to the armies of
Israel, and said to them, "Why have you come out to line
up for battle? Am I not a Philistine, and you the servants
of Saul? Choose a man for yourselves, and let him come
down to me. If he is able to fight with me and kill me, then

we will be your servants. But if I prevail against him and kill him, then you shall be our servants and serve us. And the Philistine said, "I defy the armies of Israel this day; give me a man, that we may fight together. When Saul and all Israel heard these words of the Philistine, they were dismayed and greatly afraid. Now David was the son of that Ephrathite of Bethlehem Judah, whose name was Jesse, and who had eight sons. And the man was old, advanced in years, in the days of Saul.

The three oldest sons of Jesse had gone to follow Saul to the battle. The names of his three sons who went to the battle were Eliab the firstborn, next to him Abinadab, and the third Shammah. David was the youngest. And the three oldest followed Saul. But David occasionally went and returned from Saul to feed his father's sheep at Bethlehem. And the Philistine drew near and presented himself forty days, morning and evening. Then Jesse said to his son David, "Take now for your brothers an ephah of this dried grain and these ten loaves, and run to your brothers at the camp. And carry these ten cheeses to the captain of their thousand, and see how your brothers fare, and bring back news of them. Now Saul and they and all the men of Israel were in the Valley of Elah, fighting with the Philistines. So David rose early in the morning, left the sheep with a keeper, and took the things and went as Jesse had commanded him. And he came to the camp as the army was going out to the fight and shouting for the battle. For Israel and the Philistines had drawn up in battle array, army against army. And David left his supplies in the hand of the supply keeper, ran to the army, and came and greeted his brothers. Then as he talked with them, there was the champion, the Philistine of Gath, Goliath by name, coming up from the armies of the Philistines; and he spoke according to the same words.

So, David heard them. And all the men of Israel, when they saw the man, fled from him and were dreadfully afraid. So the men of Israel said, have you seen this man who has come up? Surely, he has come up to defy Israel; and it shall be that the man who kills him the king will enrich with great riches, will give him his daughter, and give his father's house exemption from taxes in Israel.

Then David spoke to the men who stood by him, saying, what shall be done for the man who kills this Philistine and takes away the reproach from Israel? For who is this uncircumcised Philistine, that he should defy the armies of the living God? And the people answered him in this manner, saying, so shall it be done for the man who kills him. Now Eliab his oldest brother heard when he spoke to the men; and Eliab's anger was aroused against David, and he said, why did you come down here? And with whom have you left those few sheep in the wilderness? I know your pride and the insolence of your heart, for you have come down to see the battle. And David said, what have I done now? Is there not a cause? Then he turned from him toward another and said the same thing; and these people answered him as the first ones did. Now when the words which David spoke were heard, they reported them to Saul; and he sent for him. Then David said to Saul, let no man's heart fail because of him; your servant will go and fight with this Philistine. And Saul said to David, you are not able to go against this Philistine to fight with him; for you are a youth, and he a man of war from his youth. But David said to Saul, your servant used to keep his father's sheep, and when a lion or a bear came and took a lamb out of the flock, I went out after it and struck it, and delivered the lamb from its mouth; and when it arose against me, I caught it by its beard, and struck and killed it. Your servant has killed both lion and bear; and this uncircumcised Philistine will be like one of them, seeing he has defied the armies of the living God. Moreover David said, The Lord, who delivered me from the paw of the lion and from the paw of the bear, He will deliver me from the hand of this Philistine. And Saul said to David, Go, and the Lord be with you! So Saul clothed David with his armor, and he put a bronze helmet on his head; he also clothed him with a coat of mail. David fastened his sword to his armor and tried to walk, for he had not tested them. And David said to Saul, I cannot walk with these, for I have not tested them. So, David took them off.

Then he took his staff in his hand; and he chose for himself five smooth stones from the brook, and put them in a shepherd's bag, in a pouch which he had, and his sling was in his hand. And he drew near to the Philistine. So the Philistine came, and began drawing near to David, and the man who bore the shield went before him. And when the Philistine looked about and saw David, he disdained him; for he was only a youth, ruddy and good-looking. So the Philistine said to David, Am I a dog, that you come to me with sticks? And the Philistine cursed David by his gods. And the Philistine said to David, come to me, and I will give your flesh to the birds of the air and the beasts of the field!" Then David said to the Philistine, You come to me with a sword, with a spear, and with a javelin. But I come to you in the name of the Lord of hosts, the God of the armies of Israel, whom you have defied. This day the Lord will deliver you into my hand, and I will strike you and take your head from you. And this day I will give the carcasses of the camp of the Philistines to the birds of the air and the wild beasts of the earth, that all the earth may know that there is a God in Israel. Then all this assembly shall know that the Lord does not save with sword and spear; for the battle is the Lord's, and He will give you into our hands. So it was, when the Philistine arose and came and drew near to meet David, that David hastened and ran toward the army to meet the Philistine. Then David put his hand in his bag and took out a stone; and he slung it and struck the Philistine in his forehead, so that the stone sank into his forehead, and he fell on his face to the earth. So David prevailed over the Philistine with a sling and a stone, and struck the Philistine and killed him. But there was no sword in the hand of David.

Therefore David ran and stood over the Philistine, took his sword and drew it out of its sheath and killed him, and cut off his head with it. And when the Philistines saw that their champion was dead, they fled. (1 Samuel 17:3–51)

Everything about Goliath was designed to inspire fear in his opponents, and the army of God was paralyzed by fear of Goliath. The giant required the spirit of fear to accomplish his task. His appearance undermined the confidence of his opponents and stopped the army of Israel. The enemy may look well armed, but greater is He who is in you than he that who is in the world. Fear is a powerful opponent, much more powerful than any giant, but fear will always be defeated by faith.

There are giants we all face—needs, problems, and circumstances. Some of them we handle all right, but some are like giants, enemies that may threaten to overtake us. We need to learn how to kill those giants.

Lessons Learned from 1 Samuel 17:3–51

- The enemy camps not in his own territory but yours (v. 3).
- The enemy may look well armed, "but the weapons of our warfare are not carnal" (v. 7).
- They didn't know that they were the servants of God. They're in a fix because Saul was a fearful as they were. They were looking

to a man. God has not called you to be a follower of man, but the most-high God. Man will fail you (v. 8).

- "Have him come down to me" The enemy tries to get you to come down; the world system is trying to bring you down to their level (v. 8).
- We will lose if we fight all by ourselves (v. 9).
- The devil defiles us every day. Accesses the brethren daily. Might be sin, habits, sickness, divorce. Every time you turn around, there's that giant defiling you. It is encamped so strongly; we think we have to live with it. Our giants will keep us from the blessings of God. Giants of drug abuse, my home trouble, a habit I cannot control, my finances, my sickness (v. 10).
- They believed Goliath, the enemy screams to us unbelieveth, doubt and fear, and we believe the lies he tells us (v. 11).
- The enemy makes his stand—I'm going to steal, kill, and destroy (v. 16).
- We gather in the camp (church) and shout the war cry. We're going to take the world for Jesus. But we get outside among the world and become meek, quiet, and mild (v. 20).
- Circumstances override them. They saw the giant and were so afraid (v. 24).
- Know who we are—the armies of the Living God (v. 26).
- There always may be those who are more qualified than you are. All those of Saul's army were well trained. God is looking for those who are available. Have faith (v. 30).
- David went out after him. We usually read in the newspaper about a man attacked by lion, but David went after him. He didn't wait for the lion (v. 35).
- Beware of the counsel of the ungodly (vv. 37–39).
- David did not come in his own name but in the name of the Lord of hosts, the God of the armies of Israel (v. 45).
- Not by might, nor by power, but by my Spirit (v. 47).

- David said, "I am not going by my own strength. God is going to have to do this" (v. 50).
- Sometimes when we knock the giant down, he gets back up. Take the sword of the Spirit and cut off his head (v. 51).

Singing praises to God in the face of fear is a powerful act of faith that will prevail over any giant. Confidence in God in the face of fear and overwhelming odds is the source of our strength and makes us unconquerable.

Paul and Silas

> Who, having received such a charge, thrust them into the inner prison, and made their feet fast in the stocks. And at midnight Paul and Silas prayed, and sang praises unto God: and the prisoners heard them. And suddenly there was a great earthquake, so that the foundations of the prison were shaken: And immediately all the doors were opened, and everyone's bonds were loosed. (Acts 16:24–26)

Paul and Silas sang unto God, and the earth moved beneath their feet. Their chains were broken. They were set free from their bondage. When there is no hope, no light, in the time of our greatest weakness, we can still sing praises to God. Singing in a time of trial is a sign of our faith in God, our source of strength.

9. Jehovah Chereb—The Lord the Sword

> There is no one like the God of Jeshurun, who rides on
> the heavens to help you and on the clouds in his majesty.
> The eternal God is your refuge, and underneath are the
> everlasting arms. He will drive out our enemy before you,
> saying, 'Destroy him!'
>
> So Israel will live in safety alone; Jacob's spring is secure
> in a land of grain and new wine, where the heavens drop
> dew. Blessed are you, O Israel! Who is like you, a people
> saved by the LORD He is your shield and helper and
> your glorious sword. Your enemies cower before you, and
> you will trample down their high places. (Deuteronomy
> 33:26–29)

Jehovah-Cherub, the Lord the Sword—if we act and do right in His eyes,
He will be a sword on our behalf, but if we do wrong, He can be a sword
against us.

The Old Testament is all about actions and their consequences. Our
God will stop at nothing to bring us back to Him. His love is unconditional.
Verse 33 reads, "He will draw out His sword and pursue us, ruining our
land, destroying our cities in order that we might be saved." When He
slew them, they sought Him.

Judges 7 records the story of Gideon and his 300 men who holding
not swords but torches and trumpets put the entire Midianite camp into
a disorderly flight; the scripture says God "set every man's sword against
his companion throughout the whole camp." The Israelites were delivered
from their foes by God's miracle; His sword will deliver us too.

His sword can cut through every defense our enemy can raise. When
handled by a servant of God, nothing can withstand its ability to cut
straight to the core of a matter and uncover the truth. As soldiers in God's
army, we have the duty to use His Word to discern the truth and follow
it. Swords are used for close combat. Paul lists only one weapon in the

book of Ephesians because we need only one weapon, the Word, which cannot be defeated. With only that sword, we fight our enemies head-on. The battle is real, and it's right in front of us.

10. Jehovah Gador Milchamah— The Lord Mighty in Battle

A Psalm of David. The earth is the Lord's, and all its fullness, the world and those who dwell therein. For He has founded it upon the seas, and established it upon the waters. Who may ascend into the hill of the Lord? Or who may stand in His holy place? He who has clean hands and a pure heart, who has not lifted up his soul to an idol, nor sworn deceitfully. He shall receive blessing from the Lord, And righteousness from the God of his salvation. This is Jacob, the generation of those who seek Him, who seek Your face. Selah

Lift up your heads, O you gates! And be lifted up, you everlasting doors! And the King of glory shall come in. Who is this King of glory? The Lord strong and mighty, The Lord mighty in battle. (Psalm 24:1–8)

What the Bible Teaches Us

And when the servant of the man of God was risen early, and gone forth, behold, a host compassed the city both with horses and chariots. And his servant said unto him, Alas, my master! how shall we do? And he answered, fear not: for they that be with us are more than they that be with them. And Elisha prayed, and said, LORD, I pray thee, open his eyes, that he may see. And the LORD opened the eyes of the young man; and he saw: and, behold, the mountain was full of horses and chariots of fire round about Elisha. (2 Kings 6:15–17)

You and I are surrounded by horses and chariots of fire. No need to worry or faint.

> When thou goest out to battle against thine enemies, and
> seest horses, and chariots, and a people more than thou,
> be not afraid of them: for the LORD thy God is with
> thee, which brought thee up out of the land of Egypt.
> (Deuteronomy 20:1)

> And all this assembly shall know that the LORD saveth
> not with sword and spear: for the battle is the Lord's, and
> he will give you into our hands. (1 Samuel 17:47)

It is not merely that He will fight our battles; it's that our battles are His. We don't want to have battles of our own; they must be His. The Lord is as mighty in battle as He will be on the last day, when the kings of the earth shall make war on Him. He will overcome them, and the beast and the false prophet will be cast alive into the lake of fire. The remnant will be slain with the sword of His mouth. The Captain of salvation gives His people a weapon to pull down strongholds and makes them more than conquerors.

The Lord Is an Expert Warrior

He knows how to marshal His host because He is a mighty warrior. He can shake the heavens and mountains with His voice. He makes the earth fear and the inhabitants thereof to melt so that the men of might shall not find their hands. He can make emperors as stubble to His bow and mighty kings as chaff before His whirlwind.

The Lord is a victorious and prevailing warrior; He bears long before He stirs up Himself like a man of war; He is not quickly provoked. But when He rises up, He devours at once.

> The Lord shall go forth as a mighty man, He shall stir
> up jealousy like a man of war: He shall cry, yea, roar;
> He shall prevail against His enemies. I have long time
> holden my peace; I have been still, and refrained myself:
> now will I cry like a travailing woman; I will destroy and
> devour at once. (Isaiah 42:13–14)

He led Joshua forth as an armed man against the Canaanites (Joshua 1:9). He is called "the God of the armies of Israel" (1 Samuel 17:45).

The Lord mighty in battle—every battle, all battles. If there is a battle and you stay with Him, you will win with Him. For the battle is the Lord's, not yours.

11. Jehovah Ganan—The Lord Our Defense

> For the LORD is our defense; and the Holy One of Israel
> is our king. (Psalm 89:18)

The Lord our defense—this has to do with our relationship with God, our relationship of His lordship, and our being a subject of His. It is a formal relationship, one with obligations on both sides.

The Hebrew word translated "defense" in Psalm 89:18 means "shield."

The Shield of Faith

> Above all, taking the shield of Faith, wherewith ye shall
> be able to quench all the fiery darts of the wicked one.
> (Ephesians 6:16)

You have a shield of faith that will stop the devil in his tracks and will quench all the fiery darts of the enemy. The strength of this shield is related to our trust in and obedience to the most high God.

Important Scriptures about Faith

- The Just shall live by faith. (Habakkuk 2:4)
- But without faith it is impossible to please him. Study to show thy self-approved of God. (Hebrews 11:6)
- With God, all things are possible. (Matthew 19:26)
- All things are possible to him who believes. (Mark 9:23)

We know that all things are possible with God, but why can't we see through faith that the things that are possible with God are made possible to us believers?

The Bible refers to an unbelieving heart as an evil heart. A whole generation perished in the wilderness because of unbelief. "To whom did he swear that they should not enter his rest, but to those who were disobedient."

Whose report will you believe? Believe the report of the Lord that says, "I can do all things through Christ that strengthens me" and "All things are possible to them that believe."

Romans 12:3 teaches us that everyone is given the "measure of faith" when they are born again. The Bible gives several measures of faith.

1. weak faith (Romans 4:19)
2. little faith (Matthew 8:23–27)
3. growing faith (2 Thessalonians 1:3)
4. strong faith (Romans 4:20–22): "He staggered not at the promise of God through unbelief: But was strong in faith, giving glory to God: and being fully persuaded that what he had promised, he was able to perform."
5. perfect faith (James 2:22)
6. rich faith (James 2:5)
7. full of faith (Acts 6:5)
8. great faith (Matthew 8:5–13)

This man understood authority and recognized it in Jesus. We too will have greater results if we understood the authority in the name of Jesus.

Faith without Works Is Dead

James emphasized works.

> What doth it profits, my brethren, though a man say he hath faith, and have not works? Can faith save him? If a brother or sister be naked, and destitute of daily food, and one of you say unto them, depart in peace, be ye warmed and filled; notwithstanding ye give them not those things which are needful to the body; what doth it profits? Even so faith, if it hath not works, is dead, being alone. (James 2:14–17)

I will show you my faith by my works. (James 2:18)

When will the church show the world its faith by its works? Jesus said, "Greater works than these shall ye do because I go to the Father."

Fighting the Good Fight of Faith

Fight the good fight of faith. (1 Timothy 6:12)

Trust in the Lord with all thine heart, and lean not unto thine own understanding. (Proverbs 3:5)

Cast down imaginations, and every high thing that exalteth itself against the knowledge of God, and bringing into captivity every thought to the obedience of Christ. (2 Corinthians 10:5)

Our Faith Will Always Be Tested

And thou shalt remember all the ways which the Lord thy God led thee these forty years in the wilderness, to humble thee, and to prove thee, to know what was in thine heart, whether thou wouldest keep his commandments or no. And he humbled thee, and suffered thee to hunger, and fed thee with manna, which thou newest not, neither did thy fathers know; that he might make thee know that man doth not live by bread only, but by every word that proceeded out of the mouth of the lord doth man live. (Deuteronomy 8:2–3)

Why would God send His people through the wilderness? "No ye not that these things were written for our example for our reproof." We find that the children of Israel had gone through the wilderness for forty years but God had sustained them; they had lacked nothing. He had given them mammon, quail, fresh water, etc. But many were not able to enter the Promised Land because of their unbelief.

The Bible tells us that without faith, it is impossible to please God. It also says an unbelieving heart is an evil heart. If you complain, it's because you have an evil heart. I look at our world as a wilderness; we are strangers in a foreign land. We are being tested just as Israel was to humble us and prove us. Our faith is being tested.

Faith Always Causes Us to Triumph

> Now thanks be unto God, which always causeth us to triumph in Christ. (2 Corinthians 2:14)

Faith will always bring the victory. Faith is always the victory in the midst of every storm that the enemy brings to harm us.

12. Jehovah 'Immeku—The Lord Is with You

> And the angel of the LORD appeared unto him, and said
> unto him, The LORD is with thee, thou mighty man of
> valor. (Judges 6:12)

Midian so impoverished the Israelites that they cried out to the Lord for help. When the Israelites cried to the Lord because of Midian, He sent them a prophet who said,

> I brought you up out of Egypt, out of the land of slavery. I
> snatched you from the power of Egypt and from the hand
> of all your oppressors. I drove them from before you and
> gave you their land. I said to you, 'I am the LORD your
> God; do not worship the gods of the Amorites, in whose
> land you live.' But you have not listened to me.

> The angel of the Lord appears to Gideon and announces
> to him that he will be used to save his people: "And
> the LORD looked upon him, and said, 'Go in this, thy
> might, and thou shalt save Israel from the hand of the
> Midianites: have not I sent thee?'" (Judges 6:14)

Gideon did not believe. He did not understand that the Lord was with him. He belittled himself; he made excuses.

> And he said unto him, "Oh my Lord, wherewith shall I
> save Israel? Behold, my family is poor in Manasseh, and
> I am the least in my father's house." (Judges 6:15)

But the name that Gideon's father gave him speaks otherwise; Gideon means warrior. In Gideon's eyes, he was weak, but somehow before his birth, his father had been inspired to call him warrior.

And the children of Israel did evil in the sight of the
LORD: and the LORD delivered them into the hand of
Midian seven years. (Judges 6:1)

God's plan is starting to come to pass. He never leaves us in the
darkness. God would provide a warrior for their deliverance.

An Angel Appears to Gideon

It doesn't make sense that the angel who appeared to Gideon called
him a mighty warrior after finding Gideon hiding in fear. And Gideon
did not see himself as a mighty warrior or a person of great faith. When
the angel said, "The Lord is with you," Gideon responded, "If the Lord
is with us, why has all this happened to us?" He felt abandoned by God.

Gideon's Call to Be a Deliverer

God saw something in this mighty warrior that he didn't see in
himself—strength.

And the LORD looked upon him, and said, "Go in this
thy might, and thou shalt save Israel from the hand of the
Midianites: have not I sent thee? And he said unto him, Oh
my Lord, wherewith shall I save Israel? behold, my family is
poor in Manasseh, and I am the least in my father's house. And
the LORD said unto him, Surely I will be with thee, and
thou shalt smite the Midianites as one man." (6:14–16)

We See Ourselves Differently Than God Sees Us

When God came to Gideon, He didn't speak to Gideon's problems.
He had the solutions to the problems. He didn't speak to Gideon the way
Gideon thought about himself. He spoke to Gideon's potential.

The devil will speak to us about our inadequacies, our weaknesses,
our failures, our past, our goof-ups and mess-ups. Even when we get into
areas we should not be in, the Holy Spirit will reveal to us or convict us
and tell us that is not who we are. God will not speak to our inadequacies
or weaknesses; He will always speak to our potential. Most of the time,

we do not see our potential; we see our weaknesses, inadequacies, and failures because the devil brings them up all the time.

Why do we believe the devil more than we believe God? Why do we let the devil speak these things to us, agree with them, and don't believe what God has said about us? Too many of us are defeated all the time, because too many of us don't believe what God says about us.

When God showed up, Gideon was in the wine press afraid that the enemy would steal his grain. When some of us become fruitful like that, we start letting the devil steal from us.

God Shows Up

The angel of the Lord addressed Gideon, "Hey! Mighty man of valor." Gideon looked around to see if there was anyone else in the wine press with him because he believed he was weak, not mighty. Gideon was basically saying, "Why are you talking about me like that? I'm the least of my clan, the least of my family. You don't even know what family I came from. Besides that, God has abandoned us."

At times, we feel that nothing good is happening in our lives, that we're victims of our past and our present. But God says, "Wait a minute, mighty man of valor. I want you to go in my strength because I will never leave you or forsake you." God is speaking to you according to your future potential, not your past or present circumstances. He's forgiven all that and has thrown it as far as the East is from the West.

Why do you believe in what the devil has said about you when you look in the mirror? You might not say it, but you believe it. You're locked up by it. "Oh well, I'll never have anything. Everything I do fails."

And some are afraid they'll lose whatever they have. They wonder how long it will last before it's gone, not believing God can continue to bless them and take care of them.

Jeremiah was thinking the same thing: "You called me to do this, but I'm not ready to do this." God says you're ready, but you're too scared to step out of the boat; you're afraid you'll fail. God says you'll never know what walking on water is like if you don't get out of the boat, but you'd rather sit in the boat and complain about the storm instead of speaking to the storm and then walking on top of it. It's amazing the potential you have that the devil has convinced you you don't have.

You're a Genius

The Bible says you have the mind of Christ. God says if any of us lack wisdom, let him ask of Him and He will give liberally. God is saying, "I'll download my mind, my wisdom into yours just like into a computer. Whatever you need, whatever you're facing, I'll download into you. All you have to do is ask."

But we say, "I can't do that. I'm too stupid. That's not for the likes of me. That's for somebody else. I don't have enough education to do that." Where does it say in the Bible if you have enough education, ask of me and I will give you wisdom? That's not what it says; if you believe, ask of me and I will give you all the wisdom you need.

Some of you don't want to take a promotion because you don't think you have the gifts or the smarts or the talents to do what God has placed in you to do. God has given you a promotion, but you're too fearful to accept it. When God gives you a promotion because you've been faithful in what you do, He'll also give you the wisdom, creativity, ability, and anything else you'll need to succeed in that new position.

What do we do when somebody wants to promote us? Say, "Oh no! You got the wrong person" and let fear fill our hearts? God says we have the mind of Christ; if we do, we have the ability to receive the wisdom of God, and that makes us geniuses.

Some of us can't see ourselves as geniuses; we still see ourselves as we always have, as people have always told us we were instead of allowing God to see our potential. It's amazing how many times we have said "I can't" and God was saying, "Yes, you can."

The Bible says, "I can do all things through Christ that strengthens me." I can do all things through the wisdom He gives me. Don't say you can't do that, don't be afraid of that. All you need to say is, "God, give me wisdom to know what to do."

We have the mind of Christ, so we should never have negative thoughts about never amounting to anything or not being able to do this or that. Why do we listen to them? Why do we allow them to go from our head to our heart?

If we have the mind of Christ, we are geniuses, but that's hard for us to say. We say, "I remember a genius when I went to school, but not me." That's how we see ourselves, and that's how the devil keeps us below our potential; he knows what our potential is much better than we do. That's why he attacks us so much with doubts.

Cast down Every Thought and Vain Imagination

What the devil says about us will take us captive and start playing with our imagination. That's why the Bible tells us to cast down every thought contrary to what God has said about us and obey what the Word says.

As soon as you have thoughts about being dumb and unable to accomplish anything, say, "No, I rebuke that thought in the name of Jesus. That is not who I am, that is not my potential. I will not allow out of my mouth the words 'I can't' because that's contrary to what God says. He says I can. He says I'm more than a conqueror."

Just One Word Can Change the Night of Your Life

> Simon Peter saith unto them, I go a fishing. They say unto him; we also go with thee. They went forth, and entered into a ship immediately; and that night they caught nothing. But when the morning was now come, Jesus stood on the shore: but the disciples knew not that it was Jesus. Then Jesus saith unto them, Children, have ye any meat? They answered him, No. And he said unto them, Cast the net on the right side of the ship, and ye shall find. They cast therefore, and now they were not able to draw it for the multitude of fishes. Therefore that disciple whom Jesus loved saith unto Peter, it is the Lord.
>
> Now when Simon Peter heard that it was the Lord, he girt his fisher's coat unto him, (for he was naked,) and did

cast himself into the sea. And the other disciples came in a little ship; (for they were not far from land, but as it were two hundred cubits,) dragging the net with fishes.

As soon then as they were come to land, they saw a fire of coals there, and fish laid thereon, and bread. Jesus saith unto them, Bring of the fish which ye have now caught.

Simon Peter went up, and drew the net to land full of great fishes, an hundred and fifty and three: and for all there were so many, yet was not the net broken. (John 21:3–11)

One word is enough to change our whole impact and future. If we look to the Word of God, we won't have anything to fear because it will strengthen us. A leader is to be an influence. Peter went to fish; he took some others with him. They fished all night but caught nothing—it had been a night of weariness.

God can change the night in the lives of all who are going through darkness. God will give them a Word that will change their lives.

They caught nothing. Jesus asked, "Hey, guys, don't you have anything to eat?" How do you think they answered? They were frustrated and weary. But Jesus loosened the Word and gave them direction: "Cast your net on the right-hand side and you will find a catch" (v. 6). Jesus gave a direction with purpose; the disciples had to obey the direction.

Many want to reap the fruit but not obey the Word. They don't want to obey what God says, but the blessing is upon those who obey. Cast your next to the right; don't worry—you won't be wasting your time, you won't be weary and tired any more, you won't be casting in vain. Cast your net in the right place, in the right direction; the Word of God will lead you to the blessing.

Peter

Someone in that boat could have said, "Don't listen to that man. Who is this telling us to cast our nets on the right-hand side?" But Peter must have said, "I've been through this before. God is in this."

The worst thing is when we labor but catch nothing. That's frustrating. That makes us weary. But if we have faith, we will fill our boats; God will make sure of that. Businesspeople, ministers, everyone—get yourself ready. God wants to touch your future with a word that will turn your night into day. There is a miracle here available to you if you will just believe it and receive it. One word from Him can change your work, your home, your ministry—your whole life. Perhaps you're walking but in circles; routine has taken over you, and you're tired of that routine. You pray, "Lord, have mercy. Please let it be a good day." Not even God can do anything for you. The way you're praying is the way you're expecting. If God were to do something new, that person would reject it. God does not work that way.

They drew the net full of large fish, 153 of them. Think about that. Somebody counted them. And they weren't little fish. Their size left them amazed that the net hadn't ripped.

You'll be surprised too with the size of the miracle, with the blessings God will give you. Get yourself ready—your blessing will be huge! Don't get used to tiny blessings. "God blessed me today. I didn't have a headache. I had a good lunch." That's good, but God wants to go beyond that. He wants to take us back to His supernatural. We are too used to the little things, the common things, while God wants to do powerful things, wonderful things. This is the time to be surprised with the things He wants to do. The church will be surprised by the size of the miracles He wants to do.

God is getting ready, rehearsing His church like the choir that practices before it sings. God is rehearsing the church, and the time is coming that this church will see the greatest miracles.

Jesus Sits at the Right Hand of the Father

Jesus rose up and sat down at the right hand of the Father, the supplier of all our needs. The Lord Jesus works the miracles; our needs shall be supplied by the one who sits at the right hand of the Father, the mighty God, the Son of God, the King of Kings, and the Lord of Lords.

He can work a miracle in your life. You are closer to greater things than you can imagine. The day's breaking, and we've caught nothing. What a frustrating night! But at the end of their night, they could not imagine that so much would come to them. God will give you an idea; He will open your eyes, and you will see it.

Are you believing for a very large miracle? Don't think that this is not for you but for others; miracles are for everyone who believes. If you believe, it shall be done unto you. God is raising up in this church a new generation with a net strong enough to pull in all God's blessings. It's called abundant life. We need to open our eyes and see that the blessings the Lord has for us are not small. He has great things for us all.

Cast the net to the right, in the direction of the anointing in which the Holy Spirit is flowing, to where God is pointing, to where God is telling you to throw it. Where the Holy Spirit is flowing at this time. He is speaking throughout the whole world.

God is raising up His church. In some places, the church may be small in numbers, but it doesn't matter; God is leading. He is still in control, and if we believe in Him and hear what He is saying, we will have great miracles and victory in our lives.

Mary says, "Whatsoever He says unto you, do it."

> And in the third day there was a marriage in Cana of Galilee and the Mother of Jesus was there: And both Jesus was called, and his disciples, to the marriage. And when they wanted wine, the mother of Jesus said unto him, 'They have no wine.' Jesus said unto her, 'Woman, what have I to do with you? My hour is not yet come.' His Mother said unto the servants, "Whatsoever he says unto you, do it." (John 2:1–5)

God never shows up in church without an agenda. Every time we come together, God wants to do something. Every time God shows up, He does something. Regardless, people do everything but what God says. Many people who will do whatever the doctor, dentist, lawyer, or an astrologer says no matter how crazy it seems, but they won't do what God says. If their horoscope says to stay in bed, they'll stay in bed. If it says not to go to work, they'll stay home. If the IRS says they owe $1,000, they'll pay it. But if God tells them to give their last $5 to so and so, they won't do it.

There was a time when people would do whatever God said because they believed God and honored Him. We need to learn to do whatever He says we should do. It may be that God has been talking to you for some time now to do something for Him and you haven't responded.

Mary went to her Son and said, "They have no wine." That's one of the saddest statements in the Word of God; wine is symbolic of the Holy Spirit, the anointing, and the power of God. Some people come to church to see a manifestation, a demonstration of the power of God. But woe be to us if they come to our churches and see empty water pots. There's no water to distribute to those looking for a move of God. It's a sad day when the statement is made, "They have no wine."

These six water pots held up to 162 gallons. The Jews and the Pharisees washed often; they would scrub up to their elbows. They wouldn't eat until they had washed. Jesus said, "Fill these water pots with water." Wait a minute, Jesus! We don't need water. We need wine.

There are times when God tells you to do something and it may seem crazy. You may say, "God, you're about to make me the laughingstock of this church. That's not what I need to do. I need to do something that makes sense." But God is not in the business of making sense. He's in the business of performing miracles.

I like these servants. They didn't argue. I can imagine in the church today, the servants would turn from Jesus and scratch their heads. "I think the Master must have had too much sun. We need wine, and He's telling us to fill these vessels with water. It doesn't make sense to me, and I'm not going to fill them up."

It seems we always want to put God under a microscope, but I can tell you, you could search a thousand years but just barely scratch the surface of His wisdom. His ways are higher than ours; His thoughts are above ours. The Bible says His ways are past finding out.

The church needs to quit trying to figure out God and just obey Him. I don't need to understand everything; I just need to obey Him. He's the Creator of all. If He tells you to do anything, do it because others will obey Him if you do. The ravens obeyed as soon as Elijah obeyed. Elijah could have gone to a cave and starved to death, but he did what God said he should do; he went to the brook of Cherith. The Bible says God could command a rhino to raise and harvest a crop, and it would.

Some people try to do what God told others to do; we're supposed to do what God has told us to do. If we do, there will be a miracle in the making. Some haven't yet submitted to His will. I encourage them to hurry up and do it.

Mary told the servants to do whatever her Son told them to do. She didn't say figure it out, apply logic to it, rationalize it, put it under a microscope. She said just do it. It won't be hard. How many of you would be honest enough to say, "God has been trying to get me to do something for a while"? Sinner, do whatever He says you should do. God is speaking to you to get saved or perhaps make restitution for something you've done wrong. If He tells you to give a certain amount of money to someone, just do it. Don't try to figure it out—just do it.

13. Jehovah Machsi—The Lord My Refuge

Hezekiah wrote Psalm 46 after the Lord delivered Jerusalem from the Assyrians. Isaiah 36 is the setting of this psalm, and we saw that Rabshakeh, a chief commander of the Assyrian army, had brought his troops to besiege Jerusalem. In the last few verses of Isaiah 37, we read about the angel of the Lord who smote 185,000 soldiers in one night to set Jerusalem free.

> 1 God is our refuge and strength, a very present help in trouble. 2 Therefore will not we fear, though the earth be removed, and though the mountains be carried into the midst of the sea; 3 Though the waters there of roar and be troubled, though the mountains shake with the swelling thereof. Selah. 4 There is a river, the streams whereof shall make glad the city of God, the holy place of the tabernacles of the most-High. 5 God is in the midst of her; she shall not be moved: God shall help her, and that right early. 6 The heathen raged, the kingdoms were moved: He uttered his voice, the earth melted. 7 The Lord of hosts is with us; the God of Jacob is our refuge. Selah.
>
> 8 Come, behold the works of the Lord, what desolations He hath made in the earth. 9 He maketh wars to cease unto the end of the earth; He breaketh the bow, and cutteth the spearin sunder; He burneth the chariot in the fire. 10 Be still, and know that I am God: I will be exalted among the heath, I will be exalted in the earth. (Psalm 46:1–9)

Verse 1

The Hebrews put their trust in God and declared Him their refuge and strength. "God is present help in trouble." You are not removed from

---

all of life's troubles, but you are given the whole armor of God to face problems and be victorious through God, who is your help in trouble.

Your strength is perfected in the trouble when you pull out the sword of the Spirit—the Word of God—and when you use the shield of faith. "For the weapons of our warfare are not carnal, but they are mighty through the pulling down of strongholds."

Do you think God would have given us weapons if there were no battles to win? He gives us supernaturally powerful weapons—the nine gifts of the Spirit—and He has promised to be our present help in the midst of trouble.

Verse 2

"Therefore will not we fear." Why be afraid? Throughout the Bible, it says, "Fear not." Fear only opens the way for defeat.

The inhabitants of Jerusalem were afraid. They were looking at this vast Assyrian army and listening to the threats of Rabshakeh, but they didn't say a word. What a powerful way to stop fear. Is your faith in military strength, or is it in the assurance that God is always your present help in trouble?

"Mountains being carried into the sea" is a reference to the size of the Assyrian army. The army was so huge that it could not be contained in its own country. It looked like a flood. But in the midst of trouble, God is present, and Hezekiah tells his people not to fear.

No matter what difficulty you're facing, put your trust in the Lord. Don't speak doubt and fear; recognize the Lord is present and able to help.

Verse 4

This verse talks about a river. Have you ever compared an ocean with a river? The devil tries to convince us that our problems are mighty oceans.

Verse 5

We see the result of God coming on the scene. The Hebrew literally says, "She shall not be taken captive." Don't give in to the taunts of the enemy, who would tempt you to walk out and give up without a fight. Depend on the strength of the rivers of life in you. Learn to pray in the Spirit, activate that river, and you will not be taken captive by the lies of the enemy.

When will God rescue you? Verse 5 says very soon. God is always there and on time, but many believers give up because they don't see their situations improve immediately.

Verse 6

This refers to all the other cities that trusted in false gods yet fell to the armies of Rabshakeh. There is only one, true, Living God, and putting your trust in Him is not a mistake. "The heathen raged, the kingdoms were moved." They were taken captive, but the Lord fought back, and He didn't use natural weapons.

It would take a supernatural weapon to slay 185,000 soldiers in one night. Verse 6 tells us what that weapon was: "He uttered his voice, the earth melted."

Hezekiah continued in Psalm 46 by referring to God as "the Lord of hosts, the God of Jacob." In Hebrew, it reads "Jehovah of armies." He is the head of all the angels.

Verse 9

He made this war cease; He stopped the Assyrian army in its tracks so Jerusalem could be spared. The weapons and chariots of this army were toys in the hands of Jehovah of armies.

Verse 10

Tells us to rest in the Lord. "Be still" is the Hebrew word *rapha*. He's the Lord that heals you. This verse literally means, "Be healed and know that I am God."

In the final verse in Psalm 46, God is the Jehovah of armies. He commands them to have faith in God because He never loses a battle. Put your trust in Him, and He will fight for you.

14. Jehovah Mephalti—The Lord My Deliverer

> The LORD is my rock, and my fortress, and my deliverer; my God, my strength, in whom I will trust; my buckler, and the horn of my salvation, and my high tower. I will call upon the LORD, who is worthy to be praised: so, shall I be saved from mine enemies. (Psalm 18:2)

> Many are the afflictions (evil) of the righteous, but the Lord delivers him out of them all. (Psalm 34:19)

The Lord is *the* Deliverer. No matter what comes against us, the Lord will deliver us! I derive great peace, comfort, and courage from knowing the almighty God has my back. I may suffer, I may fall, I may experience great loss, but the Lord will deliver me from all evils. That's what His Word says, so it's up to me to believe, stay of good courage, and press on toward the mark having faith that no matter what may rise against me, He is there. Through prayer, praise, and worship, the Lord will see me through!

God Has Ordained Deliverance through Praise

> Now when they began to sing and to praise, the Lord set ambushes against the people of Ammon, Moab, and Mount Seir, who had come against Judah; and they were defeated. (2 Chronicles 20:22 NKJV)

Enemies were defeated when Jehoshaphat led his people into praise and worship. Victory will come to those who praise Him.

> Let God arise, let His enemies be scattered; let those also who hate Him flee before Him. As smoke is driven away, so drive them away; as wax melts before the fire, so let the wicked perish at the presence of God. But let the

righteous be glad; let them rejoice before God; Yes, let them rejoice exceedingly. Sing to God, sing praises to His name; Extol Him who rides on the clouds, By His name YAH, and rejoice before Him. (Psalm 68:1–4 NKJV)

We will see our enemies flee in confusion when we worship and praise the Lord. When we offer God praise, He will put to flight the spiritual hosts of wickedness trying to defeat us.

Fruit of Our Lips

Therefore by Him let us continually offer the sacrifice of praise to God, that is, the fruit of our lips, giving thanks to His name. (Hebrews 13:15 NKJV)

Most of us enjoy praising and worshiping the Lord. God is after the praise that comes in the midst of great trials, difficulties, grief, sickness, demonic oppression, temptation, relational difficulties, and financial problems. We must praise Him in everything. "In everything give thanks for this is the will of God in Christ Jesus concerning you" because the joy of the Lord is our strength.

The Example of Jonah

Jonah is an example of what it means to give to the Lord the sacrifice of praise in the midst of life-or-death circumstances.

When my soul fainted within me, I remembered the LORD; and my prayer went up to You, into Your holy temple. Those who regard worthless idols forsake their own Mercy. But I will sacrifice to You with the voice of thanksgiving; I will pay what I have vowed. Salvation is of the LORD. So, the LORD spoke to the fish, and it vomited Jonah onto dry land. (Jonah 2:7–10 NKJV)

God can release from us whatever has us bound. Instead of complaining about his situation, Jonah turned his attention to God through prayer, thanksgiving, and praise.

Paul and Silas in Prison

> And the multitude rose up together against them: and the magistrates rent off their clothes, and commanded to beat them. And when they had laid many stripes upon them, they cast them into prison, charging the jailor to keep them safely: Who, having received such a charge, thrust them into the inner prison, and made their feet fast in the stocks. And at midnight Paul and Silas prayed, and sang praises unto God: and the prisoners heard them.
>
> And suddenly there was a great earthquake, so that the foundations of the prison were shaken: and immediately all the doors were opened, and every one's bands were loosed. (Acts 16:22–26)

In Acts 16, we read about Paul and Silas being beaten and thrown in prison because of their zeal to preach the gospel. While they were in prison, they praised God and sang hymns, and as a result, a great earthquake shook the prison. Do you want the chains that bind you broken by the power of God so you can get on with your life in Christ and walk in victory? If so, praise God in the midst of your difficulty and watch Him set you free.

God didn't create us to be victims but victors. We walk around with this victim mentality. "Why do all these bad things happen to me?" We need to shout to God in the voice of triumph and praise.

Five Reasons We Should Praise the Lord (Psalm 81:4–16)
1. For this is a statute of God; God says for us to do it (v. 4).
2. God has ordained praise for a testimony (v. 5).
3. God will deliver us from bondage (v. 6).

4. God will answer our prayers (v. 7).

5. There shall be no strange God in thee; those who praise are protected from Satan (v. 9).

Seven Hebrew Words for *Worship*

1. **Yadah** (Psalm 134:2): worship with extended hands.

2. **Towdah** (Psalm 50:23): yadah and towdah involve the extension of the hand; towdah includes a little more thanksgiving for things not yet received as well for things already at hand.

3. **Halal** (Psalm 113): root of Hallelujah; means to clear, shine, boast, show, rave, celebrate, clamor foolishly.

4. **Shabach** (Psalm 35:27): to address with a loud tone, command, triumph, glory, shout, shatter whatever is against you in the second heaven.

5. **Barak** (Psalm 95:6): to kneel and to bless God as an act of adoration; not a begging attitude but an expectant attitude.

6. **Zamar** (Psalm 150): to touch the strings of instruments in worship.

7. **Tehillah** (Psalm 47:6): to sing and to sing praises unto the Lord.

God's People Were Bored

> But thou hast not called upon me, O Jacob; but thou hast been weary of me, O Israel. Thou hast bought me no sweet cane with money, neither hast thou filled me with the fat of thy sacrifices: but thou hast made me to serve with thy sins, thou hast wearied me with thine iniquities. (Isaiah 43:22, 24)

> Behold what a weariness is it! You have snuffed at it, saith the Lord of hosts; and ye brought that which was torn, and the lame, and the sick; thus, ye brought an offering: should I accept this of your hand? Cursed be the deceiver, which hath in his flock a male, and voweth, and sacrificeth unto the Lord a corrupt thing: for I am a great King, saith

the Lord of host, and my name is dreadful among the heathen. (Malachi 1:13)

My people have become bored with me. Their hearts were not in it. They were in the religious rut of tradition. They were dragging unwilling offerings to the altar—diseased, weak, lame, corrupt sacrifices. They kept going to church because it was the right thing to do. No excitement, no joy, no gladness, no shout for victory. Worship was weak and lame.

At Mount Ebal, God pronounced a curse.

> Because thou servedst not the lord thy God with joyfulness, and with gladness of heart, for the abundance of all things; Therefore, shalt thou serve thine enemies which the Lord shall send against thee, in hunger, an in thirst, and in nakedness, and in want of all things: and he shall put a yoke of iron upon thy neck, until he hath destroyed thee. (Deuteronomy 28:47–48)

What terrible sin did Israel commit that brought these curses?

> Because thou servest not the lord thy god with joyfulness and with gladness of heart for the abundance of all things. (v. 47)

15. Jehovah Sabaoth—The Lord of Hosts (The God of Unlimited Power)

> The Great, The Mighty God, The Lord of Hosts, is His name. Behold I Am the Lord, the God of all flesh: is there anything too hard for me? (Jeremiah 32:18,27)

In 2 Chronicles 32:7–8, Judah is outnumbered, but Hezekiah gives encouragement.

> Be strong, be courageous, be not afraid (over 300 times in the Bible), and be not dismayed. For all of the multitude that is with him; for there be more with us than with him. WITH HIM IS AN ARM OF FLESH; but with us is the Lord our God to help us, and to fight our battles. FOR THE PEOPLE RESTED (LEANED) THEMSELVES UPON THE WORDS OF HEZEKIAH.

We are never outnumbered when we lean on the Lord.

The Enemy's Boast

> Know you not what I and my fathers have done unto all the people of other lands? (v. 13)

> Who was there among all the gods of those nations that my father's utterly destroyed. (v. 14)

The enemy says don't believe what God says.

> Let not Hezekiah deceive you, nor persuade you on this manner, neither yet believe him: For no god of any nation or kingdom was able to deliver his people out of mine

hand, and out of the hand of my fathers: How much less shall your God deliver you out of mine hand? (v. 15)

The Enemy Screams Fear

They cried with a loud voice in the Jews' speech unto the people of Jerusalem that were on the wall, to affright them, and to trouble them that they might take the city. (v. 18)

Hezekiah and Isaiah Pray

And they spake against the God of Jerusalem; and for this cause Hezekiah the King and the prophet Isaiah the son of Amoz, prayed and cried to Heaven. (v. 20)

God Brings Deliverance

And the Lord sent an angel which destroyed all the mighty men of Valor, and the leaders and captains in the camp of the kings of Assyria. Thus the Lord saved Hezekiah and the inhabitants of Jerusalem from the king of Assyria, and from the hand of all others, and protected them on every side. (vv. 21–22)

King Asa

Then Zerah the Ethiopian came out against them with an army of a million and three hundred Chariots, and he came to Mureshah. So, Asa went out against him, and they set the troops in battle array in the valley of Zephathah at Mureshah. And Asa cried out to the lord his God, and said, "Lord, it is nothing for you to help, whether with many or with those who have no power, help us, O Lord our God, for we rest on you, and in your

name, we go against this multitude Lord. You are our
God: We do not let man prevail against you!" So, the
Lord struck the Ethiopians before Asa and Judah, and the
Ethiopians fled. (2 Chronicles 14: 9–12 NKJV)

This is talking about King Asa and little Judah, the smallest tribe. This is a man who was doing good things for God when the enemy showed up—an army of a million men. The Hebrew word doesn't mean a million literally; it means a number that cannot be counted. This is a massive force. The whole terrain was covered as far as the eye could see with soldiers.

Three hundred chariots might not seem like much, but Asa had only 500,000 foot soldiers and no chariots. Chariots in those days had long, sharp knifes attached to the wheels and would go right through the foot soldiers and maim if not kill them.

The situation looked hopeless, but God turned it around and brought about a great victory for this small tribe of Judah.

So King Asa got this report just as we do at times; something happens that we weren't expecting. The report that came to the king became a very dark moment for him and the tribe of Judah. We must realize that when darkness arises, we still have hope as our anchor. We are not to be overwhelmed by what we see, hear, or feel; we are to be overwhelmed by God's ability, faithfulness, and love. We should look through the problem realizing that what we see is only temporal. We might not know when it will change, but we should know it will change and by whose hands that will happen.

I find the promises God has made that apply to my situation, and there are over 3,000 promises in the Word of God. Once I find that promise, something begins to happen in my life. I see the end, not the beginning, because His promise declares what will be the end if I have faith and hold onto it.

King Asa was serving God. He had cleansed the land of all idols and pornographic fixtures. He was a worshiper. Judah was experiencing a revival that included peace and prosperity. Then out of nowhere, their peace was shattered; they would be attacked. He looked at his resources and tried to evaluate the situation. He was afraid he was not able to meet the crisis. We can all relate to where Asa was. When we look to our own selves, our own resources, we're afraid we don't have what is needed to face a bad situation. And we have all had "all of a sudden" moments.

Suddenly, something changes. Suddenly, a situation turns. Suddenly, somebody walks out, somebody dies, something happens in the financial or the marital realm. Something happens that we didn't see coming. The report Asa got was dreary, and he despaired. He feared. He felt helpless and hopeless.

"What have I done to deserve this? This was just dumped in my lap! I don't need this right now. I don't want this right now. This is supposed to happen to others, not me. But here it is right now in my family. What am I going to do? What does the future hold for me?"

We look at our resources and decide there is not enough to handle this sickly situation. Negative thoughts begin to bombard our mind. The bad news makes our imagination run wild. The worst thoughts begin to paralyze us. We become angry and frustrated and even begin to question God. "Why did you let this happen to me? Why are you doing this to me?"

We turn it back to God and then start making deals with Him. "If you make this go away, I'll tithe consistently. I'll even double my tithe. I'll do whatever you want me to do. I'll even go to the malaria-filled jungle swamps in Panama. I'll witness—whatever you want me to do. Just make this go away. I don't want to face this!"

Well, Zerah is at the gate. "What am I going to do?" Asa, what are you going to do? He didn't run from it, he didn't hide from it hoping it would go away. He didn't close his eyes, or get drunk, or take drugs. He didn't give himself over to self-pity and depression though his emotions were under attack. He didn't plan his suicide; he didn't beat up his kids and his wife or flee to escape the problem. No. He saw the hand of God in his situation. "So Asa went out against him and they set the troops in the battle array in the valley of Zephathah at Mureshah" (2 Chronicles 14:10 NKJV). He faced his problem head-on because he knew he wasn't facing it alone. He saw an opportunity for God to be glorified. He chose life over death; he chose God.

He chose God's promises because he knew that God was with him, so no one could be against him. He knew he had a covenant with God, so he confronted his problem. He knew the God of Israel had unlimited power.

16. Jehovah Magen—The Lord, The Shield, The Sword

> Happy art thou, O Israel: who is like unto thee, O people saved by the LORD, The Shield of thy help, and who is the sword of thy Excellency! and thine enemies shall be found liars unto thee; and thou shalt tread upon their high places. (Deuteronomy 33:29)

He Is Our Shield

David was constantly on the defense in his flight from the king who sought to take his life, but the Lord covered and guarded him like a shield. Just as the Lord shielded David, He shields us.

He Is Our Sword

God is our living arsenal. He provides us all the weapons required for spiritual warfare. God's Word is a sharp sword for His children. The sword of truth is our main weapon.

The Weapon of Truth

> Justice is turned back, and righteousness stands afar off;
> for truth is fallen in the street, and equity cannot enter.
> (Isaiah 59:14 NKJV)

Truth is the most powerful weapon we have in our God-given spiritual arsenal. Unfortunately, it has fallen in the streets and has been replaced by lies and half-truths. It is time for God's people to rise with the weapon of truth and go forth in the power of His truth.

> No one calls for justice, nor does any plead for truth. They trust in empty words and speak lies; they conceive evil and bring forth iniquity. They hatch vipers' eggs and

weave the spider's web; he who eats of their eggs dies, and from that which is crushed a viper breaks out. (Isaiah 59:4–5 NKJV)

If we are to stand in an evil day, we must put on the belt of truth and walk in the uncompromising truth of God's Word.

Therefore take up the whole armor of God, that you may be able to withstand in the evil day, and having done all, to stand. Stand therefore, having girded your waist with truth, having put on the breastplate of righteousness. (Ephesians 6:13–14 NKJV)

We must realize that walking in the truth of God's Word is one of the most powerful weapons we have against the enemy with his wiles and schemes. We must have a powerful love and adherence to the truth of God's word if we are to stand against him. Satan has nowhere to stand when he is confronted with the truth.

We must accept the entirety of God's Word as His truth.

The entirety of Your word is truth, and every one of Your righteous judgments endures forever. (Psalm 119:160 NKJV)

We must rightly divide the Word of truth.

Be diligent to present yourself approved to God, a worker who does not need to be ashamed, rightly dividing the word of truth. (2 Timothy 2:15 NKJV)

Go after a life of love, as if your life depended on it, because it does. Give yourself to the gift that God gives you. Most of all proclaim his truth. (2 Timothy 2:15 MSG)

We are to proclaim God's truth in everyday language so all can experience His presence with us. We are to proclaim His truth every day at work, in school, in our neighborhoods, and in church. When we speak the truth everywhere, we build others up.

We are living in a time when we are told, "Pastors, you do not want to say this, because the church will not grow." In fact, it's the opposite. God is looking for men and women who will stand up for His truth and speak it even when it's not popular. If we are more concerned about being popular than having His presence, we will never speak truth.

Speak truth to this generation; some are thirsty for the truth. You will cause them to grow and be strong. God is present wherever truth is being spoken.

What's going on in the church today? My heart has been so heavy over the state of America. There is a whole lot of foolishness going on. And the church is participating in it. It makes me cry. If we could see the body of Christ in the Spirit, we would see a body on life support. I'm not bashing this most beautiful thing—the body of Christ, but I am telling the truth. So many Christians are struggling right now. So many Christians are being attacked. Here is the key—so many Christians are being confused even in churches.

Loss of judgment is destroying the fabric of America, its foundation. The loss of judgment affects our ability to distinguish between right and wrong, good and evil even among those who have been going to church all their lives. The Bible says, "In the last days, the people will call evil good and good evil." Wrong voices lead to wrong choices. A loss of judgment. We are a society that is trying to be both politically correct and at the same time be politically wrong. Wrong about almost everything.

That spirit of political correctness is infiltrating the body of Christ. That spirit is more concerned with not offending people rather than not offending God. I want to expose that spirit of deception that hangs over the body of Christ today.

"Many will be offended." This spirit is very strong. The Bible warns us that in the last days, this spirit of being offended will pervade as never before. People today think they have a right not to be offended, but many will be offended in the last days. And they will betray one another. Divorce one another. They think their problems will be fixed by going to another church. This way of thinking has caused the church to become like Israel. Moses left the Israelites to hear from God, and while he was gone, they made the golden calf because they wanted a God that would meet their lifestyle. They wanted to make God in their image. This is what is happening in all the churches across America. Let's make God fit our lifestyle; we'll still go to church and say His name; we'll have a form of godliness in our golden-calf theology. People who were once on fire for God have become casualties of this golden-calf theology. Preachers preach with feathers, not the sword of truth, and they're just tickling people.

First, you need to be sure you don't eat from the wrong tree. Otherwise, you may make God what you want to fit your lifestyle. You may look at other Christians and say, "Well, they do this, so it must be all right."

Truth has fallen in the streets. People became tired of waiting for truth. They became tired while standing for truth, and everybody else was asking, "Where is your God?" Even among Israel, where is He? "Aaron, we're tired of waiting. You keep saying a revival is coming. You keep telling us to stand and keep trusting Jehovah. Guess what? We're tired of it. The other nations are making fun of us."

I believe we are experiencing in America what it says in Isaiah 59:14–15 (NKJV).

> Justice is turned back, and righteousness stands afar off; For truth is fallen in the street, and equity cannot enter. So truth fails, and he who departs from evil makes himself a prey. Then the Lord saw it, and it displeased Him that there was no justice.

That is happening. If you decide to stand up for truth, you could be locked up. It's crazy what we see taking place. There is a loss of judgment. We're passing laws that conflict with common sense like allowing men in a restroom with little girls. Has your brain fallen out of your head? Twenty years ago, if you had told people this, they would say that it would never happen. But it's here because the church of the Living God has been silent! There is a silence of the lambs going on. Just like when we agreed with divorce in the fifties. And now, it has become normal. The church has once again bowed.

Most of political correctness is ungodly and is against the Word of God. What is going on is found in Romans 1: "Claiming to be wise." Claiming to be politically correct, they have simply become fools.

Truth has fallen in the streets; do you see it? The strategy of the enemy is to silence truth, which is to silence judgment and leave people confused. When you silence the father and mother, when you silence your best friend because your best friend is afraid of the truth, because you will be called a hater, a bigot. When you silence a counselor, which is silencing wisdom, what will happen on earth? When you are silencing them, you're silencing God.

Political Correctness Silences Counsel and Wisdom

Truth is the new hate speech. If you speak truth today, you could be committing a "crime." So we remain silent instead of being hated on Facebook and at work and so our kids will like us. There's a spirit of fear that goes along with this. When we're more concerned about pleasing some people while others are drowning. When we silence school counselors and moms and dads. When the enemy silences pastors, he's silencing God, for they are God's mouthpieces. When we take out judgment because we're afraid we'll be persecuted as a parent or be made fun of as a student, we are silencing God.

We have to tell our kids the truth in love, not like the eighties stuff, when we beat our kids up and kids went to church out of fear, not love. Godly love leads people to repentance. Do I speak to my teenager or not? If I bring it up, it's going to ruin my Friday night. If I bring it up at work, will everybody make fun of me? So do I speak truth or not? To conform is to be Aaron and the golden calf.

God Said This Would Happen

In 2 Timothy, we read that the last days will be difficult, that people will be lovers of themselves and their money. Now was this written for the church or for the lost? They will be boastful and proud. Disobedient to their parents, they will consider nothing sacred. They will be unloving and unforgiving. They will slander others and self. They will be cruel and hate what is good. They will betray their friends and be puffed up with pride. They will love the pleasures of man more than the pleasures of God. They will act religious. They will reject the power that can make them godly.

Don't Judge Me

One of the most popular phrases you hear everywhere on social media, from your best friend, your kids, is "Don't judge me!" Let's check it out.

> Judge not, that ye be not judged. For with what judgment ye judge, ye shall be judged: and with what measure ye mete, it shall be measured to you again. And why beholdest thou the mote that is in thy brother's eye, but considerest not the beam that is in thine own eye? Or how wilt thou say to thy brother, let me pull out the mote out of thine eye; and, behold, a beam is in thine own eye? Thou hypocrite, first cast out the beam out of thine own eye; and then shalt thou see clearly to cast out the mote out of thy brother's eye. (Matthew 7:1–5)

Don't tell your kids or your neighbor not to do something you're guilty of doing. The Word of God doesn't say we are not to judge others. Paul was rebuking the church.

> Dare any of you, having a matter against another, go to law before the unjust, and not before the saints? (If you are going to take something to believers, they are going to have to judge). Do ye not know that the saints shall judge the world? and if the world shall be judged by you, are ye unworthy to judge the smallest matters? Know ye not that we shall judge angels? How much more things that pertain to this life? If then ye have judgments of things pertaining to this life, set them to judge who are least

esteemed in the church. (So, you should be able to settle ordinary disputes in this life) I speak to your shame. Is it so, that there is not a wise man among you? No, not one that shall be able to judge between his brethren? (1 Corinthians 6:1–5 NKJV)

Paul was telling us we need to judge these matters.

A World without Judgment

Parents have made a mistake by judging their kids while they're doing the same thing their kids are doing. Judging somebody at the workplace while they're doing the same thing. Before we sit at the Lord's table, we should examine ourselves. It's very important that we don't throw stones, that we speak truth in love.

Can you imagine a world without judgment? It's happening. Could you imagine America without judgment? Not being able to distinguish between good and evil, what's wrong and what's right? It's happening. Common sense is no longer common when we allow men to go into restrooms with little girls. You're a hater. No. I have a brain, and we are to judge.

Now I beseech you, brethren, mark them which cause divisions and offences contrary to the doctrine which ye have learned; and avoid them. For they that are such serve not our Lord Jesus Christ, but their own belly; and by good words and fair speeches deceive the hearts of the simple. (Romans 16:17–18)

They deceive innocent people with their smooth talk. The Bible says we will know them by their fruit. We have to judge and discern. Some may say judging is condemning, but judgment comes from God. Where would we be without godly court systems? What would happen to your child if you didn't say, "Don't go out there and play on the road"?

"Therefore, come out from among them that are not believers." How do you do that unless you're able to judge? Separate yourself from them.

Don't touch their filthy stuff. It doesn't mean you walk around self-righteously when you do so.

I Won't Judge You

A young man walked into a Bible study in a church, sat through the Bible study, then killed a pastor and everybody else there. They asked his roommate (this is where we are with this generation), "How could somebody do such a horrible act?" The roommate said, "I did hear Dillon say he wanted to kill people and start a civil war. But who am I to judge him?"

People, I know what I would do, but I'm not going to judge you. You just have been silenced from setting somebody else free; the truth will set them free.

Do you see what's going on? Be quiet. Don't say anything. Don't you know that will start an argument? Pastor, don't say that. Body of Christ, be quiet. Just go to church, do your thing, and be silent for the rest of the week. I might offend somebody; that's not politically correct. I shouldn't say that. I shouldn't refer to that. Don't condemn me. Jesus said, "I did not come into the world to condemn," so why are you condemning me? You need to worry about your own stuff. What we're trying to do is bring correction, but you're twisting truth and calling it condemnation.

That's what's going on. Correction, wisdom, and truth are silent because they're called condemnation: "Don't judge me, man." This produces Christians who walk in fear, friends who are afraid to tell friends they're going down the wrong road. But I will just worry about myself and I can pray for them.

Let me tell you, if I'm about to walk of a cliff, somebody needs to tell me. When are we going to speak up to friends, family, people at school or work who are about to fall off a cliff? The devil is silencing judgment, silencing Christians.

Parents, you need to open your mouth and quit trying to be best friends with your children. They will come back someday and thank you for telling them the truth. That best friend may leave you for six months but then may come back and say, "Thank you for telling me the truth." Somebody will be set free today because of truth. Open your mouth. It's time for the church to get healed from spiritual laryngitis. It's time for the church to get its voice back. Parents, speak up. Clean your house. Let the devil know he's messed with the wrong family. Be led by the Spirit; if you don't, you'll try to correct your kids the way your parents corrected you.

If you're being led by the Spirit, it doesn't matter if your child is a homosexual or lesbian. It doesn't matter how far your family is; God is able. Don't silence truth. Speak in love. If you don't open your mouth, guess who wins? People don't want to hear what's right anymore.

> Hearken unto thy father that begat thee, and despise not thy mother when she is old. Buy the truth, and sell it not; also wisdom, and instruction, and understanding. The father of the righteous shall greatly rejoice: and he that begetteth a wise child shall have joy of him. Thy father and thy mother shall be glad, and she that bare thee shall rejoice. (Proverbs 23:22–25)

If your children are out of your house, in the name of Jesus take them back. It's never too late to stand for truth. They're your seed. You have authority over your kids, so tell hell to take its hands off your kids. Children will never be free as long as their parents are silent. It stops discipleship and personal growth in people. People will marry outside God's will because they won't listen to leadership. You've been looking for love in all the wrong places. Because you don't know who you are in Christ, you're settling for a peanut butter and jelly sandwich when God has a steak for you.

It causes people to get mad and offended and leave church. They will find five people just like them to hang out with and start their own church. Half of all churches were started through rebellion. God will never bless those in rebellion until they repent. It stops discipleship, it stops growth; people will not listen to leaders. Wives will not listen to their husbands; husbands will not listen to their wives. Children will not respect their parents; people will miss their destiny.

The church cannot bow to the forces of darkness. If ever the church of the Living God needed to rise up, it's now. We must repent and return to God. We must repent as parents for living in fear and not in truth to our children today so God will show up in our homes. We must repent for allowing the enemy—politically incorrect spirits—into this culture. Someone needs to rip off the masking tape today and say, "I will stand up for truth. I will not have my grandkids one day ask, 'Granddaddy, why did you not speak the truth?'"

Acts 18:9 (NKJV) says, "Do not be afraid, but speak, and do not be silent." Who will stand for truth? The enemy is exposed; it is being defeated. The head of the giant is cut off today. In your family, in your house, in your marriage, you're holding the head of Goliath in your hands. The good news is that if you need forgiveness, forgiveness is here; if you need healing, healing is here; if you need to get your boldness back, the Holy Spirit is here.

We are responding more out of our flesh than out of our spirit. There are too many responses to what we see going on in America and the world; we see responses from believers and unbelievers that sometimes shock me. Responses to anything should be in accordance with the Word of God, not what we watch on CNN, Fox, ABC, CBS, or anything else we're watching. We're responding more out of our flesh than out of our spirit. Not everything we see on TV is true, but everything we read in the Bible is true; we know God never lies. Every response we are to have as Christians is in the Word. We need to be led by the Spirit, not the flesh.

When we listen to all this stuff going on, it can stir us up. The Bible says be angry but sin not. The Bible says don't let the sun go down on your wrath. The Bible also says that vengeance is the Lord's. God will bring justice where there is none. God is longsuffering. We should look before we speak or act. If we say things out of the flesh, we need to repent of that. When we blow up on our spouses and kids, we need to repent. After we repent, we should ask the Lord to help us with this. We don't want to be angry. We shouldn't say things that will bring hurt or regret to someone.

17. Jehovah Ma'oz and Jehovah Metshodhathi—The Lord My Fortress

> O LORD, my strength, and my fortress, and my refuge in the day of affliction, the Gentiles shall come unto thee from the ends of the earth, and shall say, surely our fathers have inherited lies, vanity, and things wherein there is no profit. (Jeremiah 16:19)

> The LORD is my rock, and my fortress, and my deliverer; my God, my strength, in whom I will trust; my buckler, and the horn of my salvation, and my high tower. 3 I will call upon the LORD, who is worthy to be praised: so, shall I be saved from mine enemies. (Psalm 18:2)

> Be thou my strong habitation, whereunto I may continually resort: thou hast given commandment to save me; for thou art my rock and my fortress. (Psalm 71:3)

Fortress

Any fortified place—a fort, a castle, a stronghold—is a place of defense against the enemy's darts. A fortress makes invasion difficult. Spiritually, it is a hedge of protection built around an object of interest.

A fortress is a stronghold from which you can fight. After you have been in a refuge for some time and you are now prepared for battle, the place of refuge can become your fortress. A fortress is where you are to put on your armor, consolidate your strengths, and go to battle. The almighty God is my refuge, my fortress.

David recognized that when he said, "Thousands may fall at my right hand and ten thousand on the left but evil shall not come near me" (Psalm 91:7). He wrote that if someone dwells in the secret place of the Most High and abides under the shadow of the Almighty, He becomes for you a fortress.

David discovered this truth and asked God to be his strong habitation. No wonder the Bible says, "Because you have made the Lord your habitation, there shall no evil befall you" (Psalm 91:9–10).

God Provides a Hedge of Protection for Those Who Honor Him

The word *hedge* in the Bible describes something more substantial than a bush. The Hebrew word really means "wall." A hedge was a defensive wall built around a city. The general idea of a hedge is that of a protective fence, a barrier.

In his conversation with God, Satan pointed out that God had built a spiritual hedge around Job, his family, and his possessions. Job couldn't see the hedge, but Satan could. God provides a spiritual barrier around His servants to protect them from spiritual attacks. I believe there is a hedge around every believer today, and I don't think Satan can touch anyone unless God permits it. And if God permits it, it will be for His purpose.

When Paul talked about putting on the whole armor of God in Ephesians, he was showing us the divine provision for us to become fortresses.

The Battle

> Be sober, be vigilant, because your adversary the Devil, as a roaring Lion, walketh about, seeking whom he may devour; who resist steadfast in the faith. (1 Peter 5:8)

We are provided with all the armor we need as Christians to win the battles of life. God's armor guarantees strength and doesn't leave Christians defenseless. God has given Christians armor for defense and offense—for warfare. Jesus said that even "the gates of Hell cannot prevail against his church."

Saul's Armor

King Saul told David, "Use my armor." It didn't fit David, so he rejected it. Christians have tailored armor through the Holy Spirit. They don't use someone else's armor just as they don't borrow somebody else's faith. God wants you to go out and win the victories that you have to face.

The Sword of the Spirit

> And the Sword of the Spirit which is the Word of God. (Ephesians 6:17)

You can never win by the flesh, only by the Spirit. "For its not by might, nor by power, but by my Spirit saith the Lord." The problem with so many Christians is that they fight with their mouths or muscles; God wants us to "take the Sword of the Spirit."

The Helmet of Salvation

> And take the helmet of Salvation. (Ephesians 6:17)

> But let us, who are of the day, be sober, putting on the breastplate of Faith and Love: And for an helmet, the Hope of Salvation. (1 Thessalonians 5:8)

The helmet covers the mind: The natural mind must be covered by the helmet of Salvation. It must be renewed.

> And be not conformed to this world; but be ye transformed by the renewing of your mind. (Romans 12:2)

The Shield of Faith

> Above all, taking the shield of Faith, wherewith ye shall be able to quench all the fiery darts of the wicked one. (Ephesians 6:16)

The Fiery Darts of the Wicked

The Greek word *dunamis* denotes explosive power; it's where we get the word *dynamite*. Ephesians 6:16 could be translated, "Above all, taking the shield of faith, by which you will be dynamically empowered." You become empowered "to quench all the fiery darts of the wicked."

The word *quench* in this verse is the Greek word *sbennumi*; it refers to the water-soaked shield of Roman soldiers. Before they went to battle, they soaked their shields in water so they would not be burned when hit by fiery darts.

Romans 10:17 says that our faith is increased by hearing the Word of God. In Ephesians 5:26, the Word of God is likened to water. As we submit to the Word of God, we soak our faith with the Word so it can withstand the enemy's fiery darts even if they strike our bodies, hearts, minds, or emotions.

God's Promise to Protect His Servants

> His faithfulness will be your shield and your rampart ... If you make the Most High your dwelling—even the Lord who is my refuge—then no harm will befall you, no disaster will come near your tent. For he will command his angels concerning you to guard you in all your ways. (Psalm 91:4, 10–11.)

Shod with Victory

> And your feet shod with the preparation of the Gospel of Peace. (Ephesians 6:15)

> Thou shalt tread upon the Lion and adder: the young lion and the dragon shalt thou trample under feet. (Psalm 91:13)

> Every place where on the soles of your feet shall tread shall be yours. (Deuteronomy 11:24)

We are shod with victory. Our enemies belong under our feet.

Breastplate of Righteousness

Stand therefore, having your loins girt about with truth, and having on the breastplate of righteousness. (Ephesians 6:14)

The breastplate of righteousness covers the heart. Christian soldiers are victorious through righteousness and truth that will conquer all storms, giants, mountains, and trials.

Loins Girt with Truth

Stand therefore, having your loins girt about with truth, and having on the breastplate of righteousness. (Ephesians 6:14)

The belt that holds everything together is eternal, reliable truth. We are "girt about with truth" not lies. Lies will not prevail; truth will stand.

A Girdle of Strength

It is God that girdeth me with strength, and maketh my way perfect (Psalm 18:32)

For thou hast girded me with strength to battle: Them that rose up against me thou subdued under me. (2 Samuel 22:40)

The Power of Prayers

Praying always with all prayer and supplication in the Spirit, and watching thereunto with all perseverance and supplication for all saints. (Ephesians 6:18)

Jude said, "Building up your most Holy Faith. Praying in the Spirit." You want more Faith? Pray in the Spirit.

Consistency of Prayer

Persevere—never give up, endure to the end of the battle, until there is an answer. Supplication is the enduring power that can reach into God's resources.

Jesus said, "Could you not tarry with me for one hour, the spirit is willing but the flesh is weak." If you pray with God one hour every day, you will have a touch of the supernatural all day. When you have been in the presence of God for just an hour, carnality will be a thing of the past and the supernatural will be a thing of the present.

18. Jehovah Tsori—O Lord My Strength

> Let the words of my mouth, and the meditation of my
> heart, be acceptable in thy sight, O LORD, my strength,
> and my redeemer. (Psalm 19:14)

It does not say the Lord is the *source* of my strength; it says the Lord *is* my strength. All that I have that is strong is in Him.

A rock gives stability. There is no need for stability until a storm comes. Remember Jesus's parable.

> Therefore, whosoever heareth these sayings of mine, and
> doeth them, I will liken him unto a wise man, which
> built his house upon a rock: And the rain descended,
> and the floods came, and the winds blew, and beat upon
> that house; and it fell not; for it was founded upon a rock.
>
> And every one that heareth these sayings of mine, and
> doeth them not, shall be likened unto a foolish man,
> which built his house upon the sand: And the rain
> descended, and the floods came, and the winds blew,
> and beat upon that house; and it fell: and great was the
> fall of it. (Matthew 7:24–27)

There was no apparent difference between the houses until the storm came and they were tested. The wise man knew trials would come. I have trusted in Jesus and found Him to be that rock that will hold you up in the most difficult times. When it feels like you don't know which way to turn. Without God, when the flood comes you will be carried away by the force of the events in your life.

> GOD is my STRENGTH, GOD is my song, and, yes!
> GOD is my salvation. This is the kind of God I serve.
> (Exodus 15:2 MSG)

But those who wait upon GOD get fresh STRENGTH. They spread their wings and soar like eagles, they run and don't get tired. (Isaiah 40:31 MSG)

I CAN DO ALL THINGS THROUGH CHRIST WHO STRENGTHENS ME. (Philippians 4:13 NKJV)

WHATEVER I HAVE, WHEREVER I AM, I can make it through anything IN THE ONE WHO MAKES ME WHO I AM. (Philippians 4:13 MSG)

19. Jehovah 'Uzam—The Lord Their Strength

> But the salvation of the righteous is of the LORD: He is their strength in the time of trouble. And the LORD shall help them, and deliver them: He shall deliver them from the wicked, and save them, because they trust in Him. (Psalm 37:39–40)

> Elijah—The Lord who is strong, will make you strong. (1 Kings 17:1–3)

God wants to enter your life and give you a strength you never had before. If you want to talk to Ahab, you better be strong. If you want to confront prophets of Baal, you better be strong. If you want to pastor a church full of backslidden people, you better be strong.

The word Elijah means "the Lord who is strong." The word *tishbite* means "he who make captive," so "The Lord will make you strong to hold captive the things that held you captive."

The tishbite didn't belong to the inner circle of the twelve tribes; Elijah was an outsider. But God takes outsiders, people others would never choose, and uses them.

God didn't call you to deal with little devils; he called you to deal with Ahab. Forget Jezebel. Jezebel became Jezebel only because of a gutless husband. Pastor, the only reason you have a Jezebel in your church is because she has stolen your authority and you don't know.

Elijah spoke to Ahab. It's about time leaders start speaking to principalities. The spirit of Elijah went after Ahab; he went after the king. He didn't go after the parliament, the senate, or the elders; he went after the king. It's about time that in the name of Jesus, leaders go after kings and principalities that have come against their churches, people, marriages, and cities.

Elijah was saying that the Lord would make us strong enough to hold captive the things that had held us captive.

Take Your Stand

If you are seated in heavenly places with Jesus, doesn't that mean you have authority in the heavenlies? The prince and the power of the air—isn't that considered the heavenlies? Are not principalities and powers also considered angels and demons in the Word of God?

"There shall not be dew nor rain these years, according to my word." It doesn't say "God's Word"; it says "my word." When you stand before God, what happens does not happen because of God's Word but because of your word. When you stand before God, your word becomes His Word.

Elijah said there would be no rain because of his word. Where are the Elijahs in our churches who will say, "There will not be abortion or homosexuality, the economy will turn around, and the devil will not take my children according to my word"?

Every Sunday, we should declare, "This is my word to my community—be saved, healed, and delivered." But how can there be deliverance in the community when we don't know what our word is? Give the world your word, "You serpents of divorce, you serpents of alcoholism, you cannot have demonism over my family or my community."

20. Jehovah Hoshe'ah—The Lord Saves

The LORD hears thee in the day of trouble; the name of
the God of Jacob defends thee; Send thee help from the
sanctuary, and strengthen thee out of Zion; Remember
all thy offerings, and accept thy burnt sacrifice; Selah.
Grant thee according to thine own heart, and fulfill all thy
counsel. We will rejoice in thy salvation, and in the name
of our God we will set up our banners: the LORD fulfills
all thy petitions. Now know I that the LORD saveth his
anointed; he will hear him from his holy heaven with the
saving strength of his right hand. Some trust in chariots,
and some in horses: but we will remember the name of
the LORD our God. They are brought down and fallen:
but we are risen, and stand upright. Save, LORD: let the
king hear us when we call. (Psalm 20:1–9)

The Lord Saves His Anointed

This psalm is different because it's the voice of a multitude that prays
on behalf of the King David of Israel as he is ready to go into battle. The
multitude responds to the king's prayer with the cry, "May the Lord
answer you in the day of trouble."

Answer you in the day of trouble ... defend you ... send you help ...
strengthen you. King David was about to lead Israel into battle; the
language is full of references appealing to the Lord as the God of Israel.
"But we will remember the name of the Lord our God." David put his
trust in the character and faithfulness of God, who was stronger than
chariots and horses.

David's trusting in God worked; those who trusted in chariots and
horses fell. Those who remembered the name of the Lord stood upright.

Interceding for Your Nation

> I exhort therefore, that, first of all, supplications, prayers, intercessions, and giving of thanks, be made for all men; for kings, and for all that are in authority; that we may lead a quiet and peaceable life in all godliness and honesty. For this is good and acceptable in the sight of God our savior; who will have all men to be saved, and to come unto the knowledge of the truth. (1 Timothy 2:1–4)

The Word says, "I exhort therefore," that is, first of all. Before we pray for our children, pray for kings, and all who are in authority so we may lead quiet, peaceful lives in godliness and honesty. Will God bless our leaders even though they are not saved? Yes. Why will He bless them? Because He is interested in us.

> And I sought for a man among them, that should make up the hedge, and stand in the gap before me for the land, that I should not destroy it, but I found none. Therefore, have I poured out mine indignation upon them. (Ezekiel 22:30–31)

Abraham interceded for two cities. Here, God is talking about a nation. If He could have found one man who would have stood in the gap, who would have interceded on behalf of the nation, judgment would not have come.

21. Jehovah 'Izoz Hakaboth—The Lord Strong and Mighty

> Lift up your heads, O ye gates; and be ye lift up, ye everlasting doors; and the King of glory shall come in. Who is this King of glory? The LORD strong and mighty, the LORD mighty in battle. Lift up your heads, O ye gates; even lift them up, ye everlasting doors; and the King of glory shall come in. Who is this King of glory? The LORD of hosts, he is the King of glory. Selah. (Psalm 24:7–10)

God, armed and battle ready, the King of Glory, is coming. Wake up, you sleepy city, you sleepy people, because the King of Glory is ready to enter. We have to wake up; it's so easy to get tired. We sleep even serving church. We nod off in the choir. The enemy comes to steal, to wear the saints out. There is no way we can make it without the strength of the Holy Spirit.

The Eleventh Hour

> For the Kingdom of Heaven is like unto a man who is an householder, which went out early in the morning to hire laborers into his vineyard. And when he had agreed with the laborers for a penny a day, he sent them into his vineyard. And he went out about the third hour, and saw others standing idol in the marketplace. And he said unto them; go ye also into the vineyard, and whatsoever is right I will give you. And they went their way. And again, he went about the sixth hour, and did likewise.
>
> AND ABOUT THE ELEVENTH HOUR HE WENT OUT, (about five in the afternoon) AND FOUND OTHERS STANDING IDOL, AND SAID UNTO THEM, WHY STAND YOU HERE ALL THE DAY

IDOL? They say unto him, because no man has hired us. He said unto them, go ye also into the vineyard, and whatsoever is right, then you shall receive. So, when evening was come, the Lord of the vineyard said unto his steward, call the laborers, and give them their hire, beginning from the last unto the first. And when they came who were hired about the eleventh hour, they received everyman a penny (about 40 dollars). And when the first came, they supposed that they should have received more, and they likewise received everyman a penny. And when they received it they murmured against the Goodman of the house. (Matthew 20:1–9)

Verse 6 reads, "About the eleventh hour, he went and found others standing idle"; it was almost too dark to work. Jesus spoke of a darkness in John that would come upon the earth, that would hinder humanity at its work.

I must work the works of Him who sent me while it is day; the night is coming when no man can work. (John 9:4–5)

Jesus was not referring to work today; we have three shifts all in lit spaces at work today. He was referring to a spiritual darkness, a cloud that would come upon the earth and hinder our work for God.

It was easier to save people and see miracles twenty years ago than it is today because doubt and unbelief have reached the point that they hinder the work of God. There were places where Jesus Himself did not do many works because of their unbelief. He asked the people to leave so He could get to work because they were making fun of what He was about to do.

God commands us in His Word to work until He returns: "Occupy until I come." Labor in my vineyard until I come back. Be good Samaritans until I come back. Make disciples until I come back.

Some animals such as wolves, bats, foxes, and snakes won't come out until it's dark. But Jesus was referring to the night that unclean things started to poke their heads out.

Today, we're living in darkness. Every magazine has some kind of comment about sex, and almost every commercial is centered on sex. Pornography is on the rise; everything seems to be centered on filth. Today, some members of the church think they can watch filthy garbage and walk away unstained. Today, people in Washington can lift their heads in pride and sit in front of a president who's responsible for taking God and prayer out of schools and say that America is no longer a Christian nation.

We have had churches in chains for their stand for the gospel, for trying to have a Christian school, and for not putting up with the junk allowed in public schools. Today, whoever has the most money or who can do the most mudslinging can win elections.

People feel they're all right as long as they're church members, but it will take more than church membership for them to get to heaven; it will require Jesus's blood to cleanse them. He's coming for a church without a spot, a church that says no to the gods of this world.

Whatever happened to Christians with backbones and convictions? Whatever happened to those who prayed about things before they went out and did them? The church is in trouble today because it's worldly. We need to do as Joshua did: "As for me and my house we will serve the Lord." He's saying, "You can go to hell if you want to, but I'll follow Jesus."

We're at the eleventh hour. The Lord is getting ready to call His laborers. Don't let all that's happening around you pull you down. The Lord said that when you see these things coming to pass, "look up for your redemption draweth nigh." The Lord's coming is at hand. It's too late to turn back time. It's too late to say, "I'll wait another day." We're living on the threshold of the Lord's return. I expect Him to say, "Come, for all things are now ready."

The Bible says that "life is a vapor," something that comes out of a teakettle and disappears in just a few seconds. Jesus said, "I must work the works of Him who sent me." We must do what God has put us here to do. Listen, church—we don't have time to fool around and put off being saved until tomorrow. Today is the day of salvation. Now is the appointed time, the acceptable time.

Some sinners have been playing around, and the devil has a chokehold on them. They need to run to the altar and get saved before they end up in hell. God, deliver the faultfinders. He said that in the last days, mockers, even church members, would get that way.

Quit worrying about somebody who hurt your feelings ten years ago. Bury that hatchet and its handle. If the devil has a hold on you, call on Jesus to break you free. Go to Calvary, let God nail you to the cross, and you will be a different person.

We're in a fight against the forces of the wisest serpent ever, so subtle that he was able to strip Adam and Eve of everything. And all we do is pray once in a while and go to the house of God a few minutes a week. It will take more than that; we'll have to sell out to the one who hung between heaven and earth.

I'm tired of being around people who want to split theological hairs about when the angel will put that trumpet up to his lips. I just want God to find me doing what He called me to do. We need God to shake us out of our comfortable nests and be at ease in Zion. We need the Holy Spirit to rock the church until we fall on our knees and cry out for the lost. Those who stand for nothing will fall for anything.

Christians Act Like Chameleons

Some Christians try to camouflage themselves to blend in. No one knows they're Christians. They should instead let their light shine.

Jesus said, "I must work the works of him who sent me." Your work is not done as long as there are those who are blind, lost, and sick. Our work is not over until everyone is found, every hospital bed is empty.

Some people look forward just to quitting time. They complain about their pay, and they want to work just thirty instead of forty hours. Are you doing what God put you here to do, or are you making excuses for not doing that? It's the eleventh hour. Jesus said, "I must go thru Samaria." He was compelled. He had to go there. He was on a clock. We too need to do what we have to do because our time is running out.

God Doesn't Fall on Lazy People

God's Spirit won't fall on people who sit and do nothing. His Spirit will fall on those who are hungry and thirsty and are laboring in the vineyard. He didn't say, "Call the lazy." He said, "Call the laborers." When's the last time you won a soul for the Lord? I'm talking about witnessing. "Well, brother, I haven't done that in a long time." Then you didn't get what God wanted you to get: "You SHALL RECEIVE POWER after that the Holy Ghost has come upon you, and ye shall be witnesses" (Acts 1:8). He makes you a witness. It's not an option to work for God. He said, "Go into all the world and preach the gospel. Lay hands on the sick and they shall recover, cast out devils, speak with new tongues."

You can get people to play baseball or come to a party, but you mention prayer and almost no one will show up. They say, "I don't have to pray or fast and work for God. I can just sit on the seat of do nothing." Some people feel it's a chore to get to church just once a week. But Jesus is coming for a church that is in love with Him, is on fire, and is working. It's the eleventh hour, church, and Jesus is coming whether we're ready or not. Life is short. We need to do whatever we can. There's no excuse for our not doing what God has called us to do.

No One Was Hired the Twelfth Hour because It Was too Late

The devil says, "Put it off until tomorrow." But tomorrow may never come. Are you doing anything positive for God? Are you busy for God? If the apostle Paul would have been on TV, he would have turned the world right side up. But TV is used today for everything but witnessing; it's not centered on Jesus Christ. When the Lord comes back, He will hold us accountable for every soul that fell by the wayside. Does it bother us to visit people who have a need? Jesus said, "I must work the works of him who sent me." Do you feel for your brother when you see him fall by the wayside, or do you like to talk about him and not even pray for him? That's not what God intended for the church. There are people in their homes all by themselves and lonely, but we're too lazy to visit them. God didn't call the lazy. He called the laborers. As a pastor, I know that motivating people to work for God is some of the hardest work you'll ever do.

Revival

Some people don't want revivals because they require some praying and some work. Churches don't act as if they want revivals; they don't want to hear the gospel. They're unmoved by the Word. Churches at ease are walking across thin ice. Some say, "I'll start fasting, praying, witnessing, and seeking God tomorrow." But they don't. They see the sick in hospitals but don't visit them.

God wants to have revival, but we don't know what revival is. Lord, let us taste a little bit about what revival is. Let us feel your Spirit move our souls. When Ezekiel went out to the valley of dry bones, he could have been satisfied with just a rattle and a shake. But he wanted life; he wanted to see those corpses come alive.

That's my heart's desire for the church. I'm hungry to see the Lord in the last hour pour out His Spirit on us. I'm tired of sinners coming to church and saying there's nothing to it. I want the power of God to be so thick that they will either run out or run up to the altar for repentance. I want sinners to be uncomfortable. I want them running to God. I want revival. I want to see it break like a dam bursting. I want to see the power of God working in the lives of those sitting back and doing nothing.

My God, is anybody hungry? Is anybody thirsty? I want it to rain, but first, there must be fire. That's God order. I want God's Spirit to be poured out. I have seen many times what God will do for us if we become hungry and thirsty enough. God help us, it's the eleventh hour, and I'm disappointed with some.

At one time, we didn't have to ask people to sing or teach Sunday school. We have all been warned how late it is. We know what time it is— time to wake up. Jesus was talking to His church when he said, "For the night is far spent and the day is at hand." He was referring to the coming of the Lord. God has shown me what He will do if we ask Him.

It's the eleventh hour. Time is running out. What will we do about it? We'll have to pray and shake heaven until heaven comes down and God's glory fills the temple. Lord, send revival. Pour out your Spirit, Lord. God, revive us again one more time and pour out your Spirit this final hour. Shape us and mold us.

It will take prayer that will shake heaven. I'm hungry to see God stir churches and show them His power. God, strip us to the foundation, strip us of anything that can come between us and you. We need revival, Lord. We need a pouring out of your Spirit. God, remove the stone in our hearts. God, let your fire fall upon us and revive us. It's the eleventh hour.

22. Jehovah Kabodhi—The Lord My Glory

A Psalm of David, when he fled from Absalom his son. LORD, how are they increased that trouble me! many are they that rise up against me. Many there be which say of my soul, there is no help for him in God. Selah. But thou, O LORD, art a shield for me; my glory, and the lifter up of mine head. I cried unto the LORD with my voice, and he heard me out of his holy hill. Selah. I laid me down and slept; I awaked; for the LORD sustained me.

I will not be afraid of ten thousands of people, that have set themselves against me roundabout. Arise, O LORD; save me, O my God: for thou hast smitten all mine enemies upon the cheek bone; thou hast broken the teeth of the ungodly. Salvation belongeth unto the LORD: thy blessing is upon thy people. Selah. (Psalm 3:1–8)

And it came to pass, when the priests were come out of the holy place, that the cloud filled the house of the LORD, So that the priests could not stand to minister because of the cloud: for the glory of the LORD had Filled The House of the LORD. (1 Kings 8:10–11)

The word translated as "glory" first means "weight": "The priests could not stand to minister because of the cloud, for the glory of the Lord had filled the house." The glory was so solid, real, and thick that you could not stand in its presence.

Moses said to God, "Show me your glory." The Hebrew word for "glory" used by Moses in Exodus 33:18) was *kabowd; Strong's Bible Dictionary* says that referred to "the weight of something." Its definition also speaks of splendor, abundance, and honor. Moses was saying, "Show me yourself in all your splendor." God said, "I will make all my goodness pass before you, and I will proclaim the name of the Lord before you" (Exodus 33:19).

Moses requested all His glory, and God referred to it as "all my goodness." The Hebrew word for "goodness" is *tuwb*, which means good in the widest sense—nothing withheld.

Devouring Fire

The word *glory* refers to brightness as in a bright light. Something's glory may be its brilliance as a shining light or fire. In Exodus, the Israelites were told they would "see the glory of the LORD," and when they saw it, "the sight of the glory of the LORD was like devouring fire that could not be put out on top of the mount in the eyes of the children of Israel" (Exodus 24:17).

The shekinah is said to have shone over the mercy seat; but only the high priest could see it, and that was only once a year. Outside, above the holy place, was the manifest glory of God as a pillar of cloud by day and a pillar of fire by night. This was a witness to God's presence. The glory of God in the sanctuary was seen only by the priest; the glory of God in the face of Christ is seen by all believers, who are all God's priests. The shekinah glory of God is in us as Christ's followers! How can we comprehend such mystery and majesty? And yet it's our privilege to show forth the shekinah glory for all the world to see.

Till Every Vessel Fill

The Jews bring in *Shabock*, Hebrew for "Sabbath." They're playing tambourines and dancing in the streets as they bring in the holy day; they are not ashamed of their God. They don't even know the Messiah and yet they're willing to get out in the streets unashamed of the Lord and worship Him before the whole world.

With guns on every side and facing death, they are still willing to stand and worship their God. People pray at the Wailing Wall at all times of day. They kneel and rock and cry out unashamed to show they are calling on the great God Jehovah. They do not turn their backs on that wall even as they walk away. It's as if to say, "God, you are almighty God and I am but human flesh. I back away in honor of you."

We should not be ashamed of the blessings of the Lord or the moving of the Spirit. We should cry out so the world will know we stand for the Lord and His blessings. God is still pouring out His Spirit. Some say that the days of miracles and revivals are over, but I haven't heard anything about God having a funeral. He's still alive and still pouring out His Spirit.

I believe there is a deeper experience that the children of God can have. How many of you have that Spirit working in your life?

> For the promise is to you and to your children, and to all those who afar off, as many as the Lord our God will call. (Acts 2:39 NKJV)

All day long, people have been telling filthy jokes and cursing God. But God is looking down at the churches and the people who have come together and are praising, blessing, and worshiping His name. I believe just like in the Old Testament when the glory of God would come down on the temple. I believe God wants to fill every vessel—us—so full that we'd stagger under the power of the Holy Spirit.

Nothing can replace the feeling I have right now in my spirit. Nothing else feels like the presence and the glory of the Lord.

> Now there cried a certain woman of the wives of the sons of the prophets unto Elisha, saying, thy servant my husband is dead; and thou know that thy servant did fear the lord: and the creditor is come to take unto him my two sons to be bondmen. And Elisha said unto her, what shall I do for thee? Tell me what thou have in the house? And she said, thy handmaid hath not anything in the house save a pot of oil. Then he said, go borrow thee vessels abroad of all thy neighbors, even empty vessels, borrow not a few. And when thou art come in, thou shall shut the door upon thee and upon thy sons, and shall poor out into all those vessels, and thou shall set aside that which is full. And it came to pass, when the vessels

were full, that she said unto her son, bring me yet a vessel. And he said unto her, there is not a vessel more. And the oil stayed. Then she came and told the man of God. And he said, go, sell the oil, and pay thy debt, and live thou and thy children of the rest. (2 Kings 4:1–7)

Till Every Vessel Be Full

The Lord desires to fill every vessel. Many times, we sing the same songs and go through the ritual of having church. We become satisfied and happy with what we have, but the Lord wants us to have a fresh experience every time we meet. God wants to fill every vessel. The picture here is oil. Seven things stand out about oil.

1. Oil Is Symbolic of the Holy Spirit Filling Earthly Vessels

We are the vessels the Lord dwells in. We find as we look at this that symbols of these vessels are throughout the neighborhood—in our churches, in our schools, and at our jobs. The Lord is saying, "Go to the neighborhoods and bring in the vessels. I will fill them with oil."

God's anointing is our care package from heaven. Jesus Christ is the Holy Spirit baptizer. How many of you have the Holy Spirit? Do you know Jesus gave Him to you? John the Baptist said, "I indeed baptize you with water unto repentance, but he that cometh after me, is mightier than me and he shall baptize you with the Holy Ghost and Fire."

2. This Oil Was Very Expensive

It was not like running to K-Mart to pick up oil. There was work and labor involved to get this oil. Some fruit had to be crushed. Work and labor brought forth this oil. If we're going to have a moving of the Spirit, there will be a crushing, a breaking of our will. God can use us when we get down on our knees and humble ourselves in His sight. He will lift us up.

We need an experience of Jordan, which means to descend, to be humble. That's the reason for baptism. Water baptism doesn't save you, but it is an act of humility.

Our old man wants to do wrong; our flesh pulls us to wrong places and gives us wrong thoughts. But when there's been a crushing, God will make the difference in our lives.

Piano strings have to be stretched to the breaking point before they can make music. God pulls us to the breaking point so we can bring forth music from our spirit. He's trying to send a fragrance to the world. Roses give off a fragrance only after they're crushed.

3. This Oil Was Used to Heal Wounds

When the Spirit falls upon us, He will bring peace and heal our wounds, sickness, and diseases. The Bible says we are sealed unto the day of redemption with the Spirit.

4. This Oil Was Given to Give Light

They poured this oil into their lamps to give off light. When you see a light in a house, that means someone is home. When you see no light, that means no one is home. The Spirit is telling us somebody is inside alive walking around. That somebody is the God-sent, sin-killing, earth-disturbing, devil-disturbing, revival-making Spirit of God.

5. This Oil Was Given to Refresh

> This is the rest with which you may cause the weary to rest, and this is the refreshing. (Isaiah 28:12 NKJV)

The desert heat can scorch skin. At 10:00 a.m., everything was put on hold. They would come along after the sun had pulled your skin so tight and give you olive oil to rub on your face and arms. It felt like stepping into a nice shower. Your skin would be refreshed, and you would go back to work. That's what the Lord wants to do to you—refresh you with the oil of His Spirit so you can get back to work. But many aren't working for the Lord because they haven't had the oil of refreshment on their spirits. He wants to baptize all in the Spirit so all can come alive.

Some of us think we've done God a favor if we go to the church once a month or once a week. But this was an oil they used every day; it was a symbol of the Spirit.

When the oil of the Spirit falls on us, it will make us feel young again, regenerate our lives, and make us go back to work for the Lord.

6. The Oil Was the Reason These Vessels Came Together

Acts 2:1–4 says they were all at one place and in one accord when came a mighty wind from heaven. Those days aren't over. God is still pouring out His Spirit on all flesh. Sons and daughters are prophesying; families are coming together through the power of the oil.

What brought unity was the oil, which brought the vessels from the neighborhood, stores, workplaces, schools—from all around. The Lord is willing and able to fill them all.

7. The Oil Was Inexhaustible

You may feel you run out, but if you go to the spout where the glory comes out, God will pour out His Spirit afresh on you and you'll have a song in your heart and a shout in your vessel.

The New Wine

> And it shall come to pass afterward, that I will pour out my Spirit upon all flesh, and your sons and your daughters shall prophesy, your old men shall dream dreams. Your young men shall see visions. (Joel 2:28)

> And when the Day of Pentecost was fully come, they were all with one accord in one place. And suddenly there came a sound from Heaven as of a rushing mighty wind, and it filled the whole house where they were sitting. Then there appeared to them divided tongues as of fire, and one sat upon each of them. And they were all filled with the Holy Spirit and began to speak with other tongues, as the Spirit gave them the utterance. (Note

they were already saved). Others mocking, said, they are full of New Wine. But Peter standing up with the eleven, raised his voice and said to them, Men of Judea, and all who dwell in Jerusalem, let this be known to you, and heed my words. FOR THESE ARE NOT DRUNK, as you suppose, since it is only the third hour of the day. But this is what was spoken by the prophet Joel. (Acts 2:1–4, 13–16)

Peter's Defense

"These are not drunken as you suppose, seeing it is only the third hour of the day. But this is that which was spoken by the prophet Joel." At the Day of Pentecost, they thought these men were drunk. But they were full of new wine—they were simply drunk on sweet, intoxicating, spiritual wine. The Spirit of God will make you so drunk that you won't be able to put one foot in front of the other, that you won't be able to stand up.

I want to talk about the new wine according to the Word of God. "Be not drunk with wine, wherein is excess, but be filled (intoxicated) with the Spirit" (Ephesians 5:18). *Filled* means to be full of joy and peace of the Holy Spirit. It is genuine, and after you taste it, you'll never be the same. It is the strongest and sweetest joy. It is the strongest and sweetest peace.

Paul exhorts us to be continually filled with the Spirit just as a drunkard is always filled with wine. Be not drunk with wine but with the Holy Spirit.

What Do You Mean Drunk?

In Acts 2:13, they said that they were full of sweet, intoxicating wine. It was new wine that did not come from a store but from almighty God, who poured out His Spirit on those in the Upper Room.

When you are drunk, that means the alcohol has taken over. But when you become intoxicated with the Spirit, that means the Spirit has taken over. God wants us to be full and running over with His new wine.

Full with New Wine

Some church members are sipping this new wine; they're not full of it. They're still fornicating, committing adultery, still playing around with the world. They're only sipping. They don't get drunk; they don't get consumed. The men at Pentecost didn't take just a sip; they said, "God, make us drunk, help us to lose consciousness of all fear. Pour it on us, Lord until we don't know how to act but by your Spirit." They lost all consciousness of fear. When you're intoxicated, you don't care who's around. Some who get drunk race around hairpin curves at 80 miles an hour because they've lost all consciousness of fear.

Some Christians act as if God were dead; they don't crack their lips when praise time comes. They won't even sing the songs of Zion. But when the Spirit intoxicates them and takes over their soul, they act differently.

I want to be drunk. I want the world to say, "These believers are drunk with new wine. They've lost their marbles. They don't act or talk as I do. There's something exciting about them."

The new wine is the wine of God, not the world. It's for the morning and the evening. It's not of the devil. I went to bars before, and I never heard anybody speaking in tongues there. At parties, when they run out of alcohol, people begin to go home. But you will never run out of the new wine. When you're filled with the Spirit, you don't act as if you're dead. The people who were drunk on this new wine, 120 of them, took to the streets, and 3,000 people were saved.

A Very Special Kind of Wine

In Greek, "wine" is *flugos*, sugar. It was the sweetest and the strongest wine you could put your lips to. It was so strong that it would knock you down. You wonder why some people fall to the floor when they're slain in the Spirit. This wine is so strong that it will knock the devil out of you, lay you flat on your back, operate on you, and clean you of worldly things. When you get up, you won't ever be the same.

This Wine Is Not Bitter

It's the strongest and the sweetest. The Bible says God hasn't given us the Spirit of fear but of power and love and a sound mind. "But you shall receive power after the Holy Spirit has come upon you."

We're living in a mixed-up generation; they need the new wine to sober their minds. Some people race to save animals but say nothing about the abortion problem. They're worried about global warming while their families are falling to pieces. They wonder what's in outer space while people on earth are starving.

It's Something You Can Drink Every Day

"Be filled every day" one translation says. Not once filled and always filled. He said, "Come and drink of my Spirit freely when you're dry. You that hunger and thirst after righteousness shall be filled." If you hunger, He will pour out His Spirit on you to refresh and empower you.

When you fall in love with Jesus, He will fill you full of His Spirit, and you'll be like the disciples when they came out of the Upper Room. There was a blaze in their lives and a sharpness to their tongues.

Today, we don't have enough of the Spirit to testify. We use dirty words on the job and in school to fit in. We think we have to act like the crowd. But when this new wine gets in you, the world comes out of you and you don't want to fit in the world anymore. This new wine satisfies; you don't have to read filthy magazines or watch filthy movies when you get the new wine. Nothing in this world will satisfy like Jesus Christ.

Young People

If some of you young people would get filled with the Holy Spirit instead of worrying about personalities and making others like you, if you would stand up for Jesus, you would make a difference. When you're lost in Jesus, you'll put behind sex and other bad things. Young people, you need the new wine of His Spirit.

I hear parents say, "I'm not going to force my kids to do anything. I'll let them find their own way." But there are too many deceiving spirits, too many detours that lead them into the hands of the devil. The devil is spending megabucks to get our children into drugs and heavy rock 'n' roll music—anything to draw them to Satan.

It's time for the church to wake up, shake itself, and catch the wave of the Spirit and the power of God as it moves across the land.

The problem with the Church today is that we drink from the fountains from this world system. You can't quench your thirst with what the world offers. You can try and try but you still are going to come up thirsty.

It's like drinking a soda drink you will never be able to quench your thirst, it cold, it goes down yummy but because it is so full of sugar you are going to have something else. Water is the only thing that can quench your thirst.

People cannot every satisfy you, you may think if only I could have her or if only I can have him, or marry this one, and we find out that nothing or nobody can quench your thirst. Only Jesus Can satisfy you because God created you to drink from His Spirit. Because that thirst that everybody has in the inside of them whether they know it or not is the thirst for the living God. That thirst to be in union and to know God and to have a relationship with God.

Come and Drink

> But whosoever drinketh of the water that I shall give him shall never thirst again; the water that I shall give him shall be in him a well of water springing up into everlasting life. (John 4:14)

> If any man thirst, let him come unto me and drink, he that believeth on me, as the scriptures hath said, out of his belly shall flow rivers of living water. (John 7:37–39)

John 4:14 mentions a well, while John 7:38 mentions rivers. These are two experiences Jesus was talking about. Somebody told me I could drink at a different bar, Joel's bar: "In the last days, I will pour My Spirit." I start drinking at Joel's bar and I get filled with the baptism of the Holy Spirit, the new wine. The well is the blessing of the new birth in you. It is the well of water in you springing up into everlasting life. It refers to salvation. The rivers of living water is the baptism of the Holy Spirit.

The Holy Spirit and Fire

Two gospels record that Jesus would baptize with the Holy Spirit; the other two say the Holy Spirit and fire. Two things that stand out in the Word of God about fire—it has the ability to attract, and it has the ability to cleanse. Fire will purify water of bacteria, and the fire of the Lord will purify you.

I was once like that water—I had filth and evil in my life. But God began to turn the heat up. He began to turn the fire on in my life. It brought conviction and made me run from the devil. God purified my spirit. He's not like a doctor who says, "I can't do any more for you."

The Fire of God Is a Motivator

You can't motivate dead people. I've seen people in church when the fire came down who didn't feel a thing. If an atomic bomb went off, they wouldn't feel it. I believe if a mosquito had bitten them, it would have flown away singing, "There is power in that blood!"

I am not a fire extinguisher. People will come to church but not praise the Lord; they don't have the fire. If you have the fire, you'll shout it every time; it won't burn out from one service to the next. When you get it, the devil can't cool you off that easily.

Jeremiah said it was a fire shut up in his bones; he couldn't stand still. David said that his heart was hot when he was just thinking about the Lord. On the road to Damascus, the disciples remembered when Jesus broke bread and they said, "Did not our hearts burn within us?"

Some of you need to be filled or refilled. All you need to do is lift up your hands toward heaven and ask Jesus to baptize you in the Holy Spirit.

23. Jehovah Go'el—The Lord Thy Redeemer

> And I will feed them that oppress thee with their own
> flesh; and they shall be drunken with their own blood,
> as with sweet wine: and all flesh shall know that I the
> LORD am thy Savior and thy Redeemer, the mighty One
> of Jacob. (Isaiah 49:26)

> Thou shalt also suck the milk of the Gentiles, and shalt
> suck the breast of kings: and thou shalt know that I the
> LORD am thy Savior and thy Redeemer, the mighty One
> of Jacob. (Isaiah 60:16)

The *go'el*, redeemer, had a particular place in Israel's social life. We read about it in the description of the jubilee (Leviticus 25) and in the wonderful story of Boaz and Ruth. The land shall not be fallow forever "for the land is mine." God had spoken, and the children of Israel were His servants.

The firstborn son in the family (or the nearest kinsman) was appointed to watch over the rights and possession of his younger brothers or kinsmen. When a relative fell into poverty and was forced to sell himself as a slave, his go'el or redeemer was obliged to redeem him. In the Old Testament, we read that the task of the redeemer had a deeper meaning than only to ransom a slave or his property; he was a higher person. The Lord, their Redeemer, would deliver them from the devil and death.

In the New Testament, Jesus Christ is revealed as the Redeemer. The book of Ruth is a beautiful, pastoral account of the kinsman redeemer, the go'el. Boaz, Ruth's go'el, is a picture of our Lord and Savior Jesus Christ, our Jehovah Go'El. Jesus redeemed His bride, the church, paying the price of redemption with His blood on the cross. Just like Ruth, who was the Gentile bride of Boaz, the church is the Gentile bride of Christ. As the Go'El, the redeemer must be a relative who is free and able to pay the price of redemption and prepared to marry the widow.

As our Jehovah Go'El, Jesus was our relative when He became flesh (John 1:1). He was free from the sin that bound us (John 8:32, 36). He paid the price of redemption by giving His all for the lost and dying souls of the world (2 Corinthians 8:9). He was willing to pay the price of redemption as so beautifully portrayed in the Garden of Gethsemane (Luke 22:39–42). He was willing to take His bride, the church (Revelation 19:6–9).

I Am Redeemed

> Christ has redeemed us from the curse of the Law, being made a curse for us: for it is written, cursed is everyone who hangs on a tree. (Galatians 3:13)

> My little children, these things write unto you, that you sin not. And if any man sin, we have an advocate with the Father, Jesus Christ the righteous. And He is the propitiation for our sins: and not for ours only, but also for the sins of the world. (1 John 2:1–2)

Some of us think God is sitting on his throne ready to hit us on the head with a stick when we do wrong. But we are more than flesh; we are somebody in Jesus Christ.

Notice the attitude of John as one of the sons of thunder. He was seventeen when he said, "That crowd is not going with us, Lord. Why don't you just bring fire down on them and burn them up?" Jesus said, "You know not what spirit you are of."

Then we find John way up in age, and his attitude about the way God handles things has changed. As a young man, he was willing to destroy anything that restricted the path of God. We hear an aged man with a voice that is cracking. It changes from "Lord, bring fire down on them and burn them up" to "My little children, that you sin not, and if any man sin, we have an advocate with the Father, Jesus Christ the righteousness. And He is the Propitiation (God satisfied with the word of Jesus Christ) for our sins." This man found something in God that he didn't see at age seventeen.

Paul

The apostle Paul said, "Oh wretched man that I am, who should deliver me from this body of this death" (Romans 7:24). This is a giant of a man crying out, "Oh, God, I am a wretched man. I'm doing what I don't want to do."

The Sons of Eli

The sons of Eli were committing adultery in the temple, and Eli made a beautiful statement: "If one man sin against another, the Judge shall judge him: but if a man sins against the Lord, who will entreat for him?" (1 Samuel 2:25). If a man sins against another man, the judge will step in and work out his case. But if a man sins against the Lord, who will speak up in his place?

> And if any man sin, we have an Advocate with the Father, Jesus Christ the righteous. And He is the propitiation (God satisfied with the work of Jesus Christ) for our sins. (1 John 2:1–2)

Job

Let me paraphrase what Job says. It's the oldest book in the Bible: "God, you don't understand what I'm going through. You never lost a son, you never lost a daughter, you don't know what sin is." He pleads with God to realize where he and all others are at.

Abraham and Isaac (Genesis 22)

Abraham and Isaac are going up a mountain, the same place where Jesus would be crucified. Abraham is about to sacrifice his son. They have an altar, wood, a knife, everything but the sacrifice. Isaac said, "Father, I see the fire, the altar, but where's the lamb?"

The word *redeemed* falls on these verses. All these questions must be answered. Eli asked that if a man sin against the Lord, who would step in? Isaac asked where the sacrifice was. Paul said, "Who will deliver me from this body of death?" Job said, "God, you don't understand what I'm going through."

Leviticus 25:25–55

Leviticus casts light on the word *redeemed*. This book has been described as a Christian cookbook; it's one of the most complicated books because it's full of do's and don'ts. Leviticus 25:25 speaks of a brother who doesn't have any money, so he sells some of his possessions, his land, and even himself. One time, I was a sinner. I was lost in my sins and didn't own anything. I was sold unto sin. This gives us a shadow of the word *redeem*.

Here is a man who has sold himself and all he had. Leviticus commanded that he go to his kinsman to be rescued and to buy back himself and his possessions—to bail him out.

I'm glad the Lord came when all humanity had been robbed and redeemed everyone.

The Roman Empire

Women were known for how many husbands they had. They were even having sex in the temple, and they were burning Christians at the stake. The Maccabean revolt was going on, the Jews were being oppressed, and Jesus couldn't have picked a better time to walk into the synagogue, pick up the book of Isaiah, and say, "The Spirit of the Lord is upon me, to set the captives free."

Say, "I am redeemed." The devil doesn't want you to know that you're redeemed and that you need to start acting like it. Get a smile on your face and quit playing at religion.

Adam and Eve in the Garden

At one time, Adam and Eve were the richest people on earth. They had everything but one tree. God had given them dominion over all the fowl of the air, over the animals, fishes, over everything that walked. "You can speak to a lion, and he will lie down like a lamb. You can call the birds to your hands and feed them. You call them by name." Some scholars think that animals could carry on conversations with Adam. But through Satan's deception, they lost all the authority they had; they traded it for a taste of something they didn't need.

First and Second Adam

The Bible says that by one man's disobedience, sin entered the world and brought death. But a second Adam came and redeemed us by His death on the cross.

John 10:10 tells us the devil came into this world "to steal, kill, and destroy." How many of you still belong to him? Are still his slave? Jesus told us, "I am come that you might have Life, and have it more abundantly." We're walking around with our pockets pulled out acting like a bunch of poor folks. But in reality, we are all redeemed by Jesus's blood.

Three Meanings of Redemption

1. Purchasing the Slave

Christ purchased the sinner in the marketplace. The original Greek means that He went out of his way, walked into the marketplace where slaves were being sold, and bought that slave. Jesus said, "Father, I am going down on earth. Let me disrobe myself, let me remove all the glory. I'll lay down my life for them, I'll pay the price for them. I'll redeem them."

"Thou shalt call His Name Jesus, for He shall save His people from their sins." The Greek word for "savior" is *soter*. He came not just to wipe our sins out but to heal our bodies and set us free. Jesus paid the price for a whole group of slaves: "All have sinned and came short of the glory of God." Jesus looked at a woman who had been bound for a number of years and asked, "Ought not this daughter of Abraham who Satan has bound be loosed from her infirmities?"

It's time for us to understand we are redeemed, we are planted in faith in the Word, and are standing on God's promises. We need to get up out of the dust and say, "Devil, I am redeemed!" Are you sitting around sick? Is sin eating your soul? You're sitting around with a hook and chain around you?

You've already been redeemed. I was locked up in the marketplace with chains and shackles on me. The god of this world had a hook in my mouth, and he was leading me to hell, but Jesus bought me out of bondage. The Master came by, saw the world, and said, "I'll die for them. I'll pay the price. I'll set them free." He redeemed all those sold to sin.

I see them all the time in the marketplace and want to say, "You've been redeemed!"

2. Taking You out of the Marketplace

Some people were bought and sold again and again. This meaning of the word *redemption* refers to Jesus's buying us, taking our chains off, and taking off our slave clothes. But some folks who are free are still sitting in the marketplace. The prison door has been opened, so what are they still doing inside? They've been redeemed by Jesus's blood!

He paid the time and He paid the price, so there's no reason for us to walk around as if we're defeated. We're free, no longer slaves in chains. Our Master has set us free. We don't belong to the evil master, the devil, anymore. We're no longer in bondage in Egypt.

Tell the devil right now, "I'm free! I've seen the Savior, the risen Lord, and my soul has been set free."

Jesus was sold for thirty pieces of silver, the price for a slave in those days. So the further meaning of *redeemed* is that the slave was never to be exposed to another sale.

3. A Different Relationship with Him.

When Jesus redeemed us, He gave us the opportunity to become the adopted sons and daughters of God. We are no longer in chains and shackles; we're now God's children!

Galatians 4:5–7 confirms that Jesus came

> To redeem them that were under the Law, that we might receive the adoption of sons. And because ye are sons, God hath sent forth the Spirit of His Son into your hearts, crying ABBA Father. Wherefore thou art no more a servant, but a son; and if a son, then an heir of God through Christ.

I have read our Father's will. I am no longer a servant or a slave; I have become His son, and Jesus Christ is my elder brother.

It took a kinsman to get us out of the marketplace. It took a kinsman to get us out of the poorhouse. He didn't come to get slaves but to get His sons and daughters. He came to adopt us and make us the sons and daughters of the most high God. The apostle Paul said in Philippians 4:19 without being bashful, "But my God shall supply all my needs according to his riches in glory." Paul was saying, "My Daddy's got it all. He's my Daddy, and I'm His son."

When He said, "I have given you the keys to the kingdom," He meant He has given us the keys to the front door. It's locked to everyone but His sons and daughters.

When your children visit you, they don't have to call to see if it's okay to come. They don't have to worry if plates will be set for them at suppertime. "If you being evil know how to give good gifts unto your children, how much more shall your father give good gifts."

Jesus directed us in the Lord's Prayer, "Our Father which art in Heaven" He's my Father, and I'm His son, and I can go to Him whenever I want. Some of you haven't caught on to this yet. Some of you don't realize who you are; you're still in chains and shackles, you're still acting like slaves when the Lord wants to make you His heirs. When the Spirit comes, He takes you out of the marketplace. He removes the chains and shackles. He sanctifies and purifies you with His blood. He brings you out of where you are.

A New Creation

Do you remember the pit He brought you out of? David said, "You brought me out of the horrible pit and put me on a solid rock, and you establish my goings." "Therefore, if any man be in Christ, He is a new creation." Metamorphosis sets in; you're not what you once were. You don't go to the places you once went. You're not in the slave quarters anymore; you don't have chains and shackles anymore. You are redeemed by the blood of Jesus Christ.

He paid the price for the slaves; He redeemed them. I don't believe in steps 1 through 4 of salvation; I believe God can clean it all at once. He makes a clean sweep when He comes.

> Who gave himself for us, that He might redeem us from all iniquity, and purify unto Him a peculiar people. (Titus 2:14)

His blood will purify you from sin and sanctify your mind. John 8:36 says, "Therefore, if the Son shall make you free, you shall be free indeed." I am free. I am not bound anymore. My Kinsman came and set me free. Romans 8:1–2 says,

> There is therefore now no condemnation to them which are in Christ Jesus, who walk not after the flesh, but after the spirit. For the law of the Spirit of life in Christ Jesus hath made me free from the law of sin and death.

John Wesley

In a vision, he finds himself standing in the presence of God at the judgment hall. As he's standing, a figure walks up to him with the blazing of hell under his hood. He pulls out a book and says, "John Wesley, you're a sinner. You're lost and on your way to hell. You remember a time when you were supposed to witness to someone but didn't. You disobeyed the Lord. God will destroy your soul because you disobeyed him."

Wesley said that as this figure began to talk to him, he stooped over and began to walk away from the throne of God. As he was walking along, a beautiful, clear voice began to ring through heaven calling his name. Wesley remembered the cross. He went to that figure and said, "There's one thing you don't have in that book, devil—Christ's blood cleanses us of all sin and unrighteousness."

Can we answer Eli's question? Who will entreat the Lord if we sin against the Lord? John said we have a propitiation and advocate in the Father—Jesus Christ, the righteous. He's my lawyer, and He will step in

AM

and say, "Wait a minute! You can't do anything with him. He's not a slave anymore. His sins are under my blood."

It's time for us to let the devil know we're not afraid of him because we've been redeemed, saved. We are the righteousness of God, and we need to start acting like it. Say it with me: "I am redeemed by the blood of Jesus Christ. I'm no longer a slave. I'm an heir of the King. Jesus Christ is my elder brother. God is my Father, and the devil is defeated. I have been redeemed. I don't have to obey the devil. I've been set free from the marketplace."

You have been letting the devil ride you. You need to get the saddle off your back. The moment you realize you've been redeemed, you don't have to take his junk anymore. You're not in the slave quarters or in the marketplace; your chains and shackles have been broken. The prison door is open, so come out. You've been redeemed.

24. Jehovah Hashopet—The Lord the Judge

> Wherefore I have not sinned against thee, but thou doest me wrong to war against me: the LORD the Judge be judge this day between the children of Israel and the children of Ammon. (Judges 11:27)

Throughout the Bible, people of every rank call for the Lord to decide their cases. We hunger for righteous judgment. Listen to the siren song, the seductive words of Absalom in the gate: "Absalom said moreover, oh that I were made judge in the land, that every man which hath any suit or cause might come unto me, and I would do him justice!" (2 Samuel 15:4).

Here he sits planting seeds of unrest, dissatisfaction, and revolution among the people against King David, his father. All the people cry for a righteous judge, but at best, only half the people can have their way with a righteous human judge. We consider our own causes to be righteous, but that cannot be. In issues between us, we cannot all be right; someone must be wrong. The people wanted a righteous earthly judge, but Absalom tantalized them with not a righteousness judge but a judge who would agree with them.

Great White Throne Judgment

> And I saw a great white throne, and him that sat on it, from whose face the earth and the heaven fled away; and there was found no place for them. And I saw the dead, small and great, stand before God; and the books were opened: and another book was opened, which is the book of life: and the dead were judged out of those things which were written in the books, according to their works. And the sea gave up the dead which were in it; and death and hell delivered up the dead which were in them: and they were judged every man according to their works. And death and hell were cast into the lake

of fire. This is the second death. And whosoever was not found written in the book of life was cast into the lake of fire. (Revelation 20:11–15)

Christ commissioned the office of judge: "Shall not the Judge of all the Earth do Right?" (Genesis 18:25). "The Father Judges no man" (John 5:22). "He has committed all judgment to the son" (John 5:22). Jesus is the sole manager of the great day of the final judgment, the Great White Throne Judgment for the lost because the Father gave Him that authority and the authority to execute judgment (John 5:27). He who pronounces judgment on them is the same who brought salvation to them.

The Wicked Dead Will Be Judged

And the sea gave up the dead which were in it, and death and hell delivered up the dead which were in them: And they were judged every man according to their works, and death and hell were cast into the Lake of Fire. This is the second death and whosoever was not found written in the Book of Life was cast into the Lake of Fire. (Revelation 20:13–15)

The Great White Throne

There will be one class of people who are going to be there—the lost. No Christian will be there.

But the Fearful, and unbelieving, and the abominable and murders, and whoremongers, and sorcerers and idolaters and all liars, shall have their part in the Lake which burns with fire and brimstone; Which is the second death. (Revelation 21:8)

Different Degrees of Punishment

> And that servant, which knew his lord's will, and prepared
> not himself, neither did according to his will, shall be
> beaten with many stripes. (Luke 12:47)

All will be judged according to their works, and there will be different levels of punishment. There are many good, moral people, but it still will be an eternal lake of fire. I'm not trying to lessen the severity of eternal punishment; the best place in hell will be so horrible that it's beyond our ability to describe it. The record books will be opened, and all will be judged according to their works.

One of these books that may be open is the Bible. It will be read to them, and they will stand there without anything for their defense. Some at the Great White Throne Judgment will offer up their own righteousness, their own goodness, and say, "God, haven't I done this in thy name? Haven't I been a good church attender and paid my tithes?" God will have another book, the Book of Life, and will look for their names in it but they won't be there. No one going to hell will be able to say he or she didn't receive a fair trial.

The Jury at This Throne: Five Sets of Books

> The eyes of the Lord are in everyplace, beholding the evil
> and the good. (Proverbs 15:3)

The judge of this throne is Christ Himself.

The Book of Conscience

> Their conscience also bearing witness, and their thought
> the meanwhile accusing or else excusing one another.
> (Romans 2:15)

Though man's conscience is not an infallible guide, he will nevertheless be condemned by those occasions when he deliberately violated it.

The Book of Words

> But I say unto you that every idle word that men shall speak, they shall give account thereof in the day of Judgment. For by thy words thou shall be justified, and by thy words thou shall be condemned. (Matthew 12:36–37)

The Book of Secrets

> God shall judge the secrets of men by Jesus Christ. (Romans 2:16)

The Book of Public Works

"I know thy works" appears seven times in Revelations.

> For the son of man shall come in the glory of his father with his angels. And then he shall reward every man according to their works. (Matthew 16:27)

Did you feed the hungry? Clothe the naked? Visit me in prison?

The Book of Life

> There shall in no wise enter into it anything that defiles, neither whatsoever works abomination, or makes a lie: But they which are written in the Lamb's Book of Life. (Revelation 21:7)

> And whosoever was not found written in the book of life was cast into the Lake of Fire. (Revelation 20:15)

This judgment is called the judgment seat of Christ.

> For we must all appear before the Judgment Seat of Christ; that everyone may receive the things done in his body (Life) according to that he hath done, whether it be good or bad. (2 Corinthians 5:10)

This is for believers only. The judgment seat of Christ refers to the judgment of believers' works.

Who Will This Judgment Be On?

This "we" refers to you and me. Paul was writing to the Christians. One day, we will stand before God, look Him in the eye, and account for what we have done since we were saved. There will be no sinners—only the saved. What Christians give up in coming to God has no comparison to what they will receive.

The Greek word for "judgment seat" is *bema*, "reward." Our works will be on trial; it won't decide if we are lost or saved. It will be a judgment to receive rewards for the things we've done since we were saved.

Works of the Believers

> According to the grace of God which is given unto me, as a wise master builder, I have laid the foundation, and another builds thereon. But let every man take heed how he builds thereupon. For other foundation, can no man lay than that is laid, which is Jesus Christ. Now if any man builds upon this foundation gold, silver, precious stones, wood, hay, stubble; Every man's work shall be made manifest: for the day, shall be revealed by fire; and the fire shall try every man's work of what sort it is. If any man's work abides which he hath built thereupon, he shall receive a reward. If any man's work shall be burned, he shall suffer loss (rewards): but he himself shall be saved; yet so as by fire. (1 Corinthians 3:10–15)

God Classifies the Works of Believers in Six Areas

1. Gold, Silver, and Precious Stones
Those worthy objects will survive the judgment fires.

2. Wood, Hay, and Stubble.
Those objects will not survive the judgment fires.

> Let every man take heed of what he builds thereof. (v. 3:10)

The judgment fires of God shall try every work. I want to be found building a structure that will withstand God's refining fires. You can melt gold, but it will resolidify.

> If any man's work abides which he hath built thereof he shall receive a reward. (v. 3:12)

> If any man's work shall be burned, he shall suffer loss, but he himself shall be saved. (v. 3:15)

There will be tears, fear, and trembling at the judgment seat of Christ. Not everyone will receive a reward. Some will be stripped of the rewards they thought they had. If our works do not withstand the judgment fires of God, we will still have eternal life, but the crowns and rewards will be lost.

Believers' Self-Judgment

> For if we would judge ourselves, we should not be judged, but when we are judged we are chastened of the Lord. (1 Corinthians 11:31–32)

True Story

One day, two young men who were racing came to a bridge. One lost control and went into the water. The other stopped his car, jumped into the water, and rescued him.

Years later, the young man who had been injured killed somebody and was brought to court. He realized the judge was the one who had rescued him years earlier. He thought, *He helped me once, so he'll help me again.*

The jury found him guilty of murder in the first degree and sentenced him to the electric chair. The judged asked him, "Do you have any final words?"

"Yes, I do," he said. "Do you remember me?"

The judge said, "Yes."

The guilty man said, "You saved me once, and you have a chance to save me again."

The judge said, "I placed my hands on this Bible and gave an oath that I'd uphold the law. You have been found guilty. I was your savior back then, but today, I am your judge."

God is loving, gracious, forgiving, and patient, but He is also a consuming fire. He takes revenge against evil and will punish us for our wrongdoings.

Don't take His silence for granted; don't mistake that for His patience with you. He is giving you yet another opportunity to change.

25. Jehovah Naheh—The Lord Who Smiteth

Moreover, the word of the LORD came unto me, saying, (2) Also, thou son of man, thus saith the Lord GOD unto the land of Israel; An end, the end is come upon the four corners of the land. (3) Now is the end come upon thee, and I will send mine anger upon thee, and will judge thee according to thy ways, and will recompense upon thee all thine abominations. (4) And mine eye shall not spare thee, neither will I have pity: but I will recompense thy ways upon thee, and thine abominations shall be in the midst of thee: and ye shall know that I am the LORD. (5) Thus, saith the Lord GOD; An evil, an only evil, behold, is come. (6) An end is come, the end is come: it watcheth for thee; behold, it is come. (7) The morning is come unto thee, O thou that dwellest in the land: the time is come, the day of trouble is near, and not the sounding again of the mountains. (8) Now will I shortly pour out my fury upon thee, and accomplish mine anger upon thee: and I will judge thee according to thy ways, and will recompense thee for all thine abominations. (9) And mine eye shall not spare, neither will I have pity: I will recompense thee according to thy ways and thine abominations that are in the midst of thee; and ye shall know that I am the LORD that smiteth. (Ezekiel 7:1–9)

I would think that the Lord who smiteth would be smiting the enemies of a godly man, but in the above passage, that is not the case (see v. 3). He is smiting His chosen people for their disobedience. His smiting is more like the smiting that a parent does to a child. It is also called chastisement.

Blessed is the man whom thou chastenest, O LORD, and teachest him out of thy law; That thou mayest give him rest from the days of adversity, until the pit be digged for the wicked. For the LORD will not cast off his people, neither will he forsake his inheritance. But judgment shall return unto righteousness: and all the upright in heart shall follow it. (Psalm 94:12–15)

Wherefore seeing we also are compassed about with so great a cloud of witnesses, let us lay aside every weight, and the sin which doth so easily beset us, and let us run with patience the race that is set before us, Looking unto Jesus the author and finisher of our faith; who for the joy that was set before him endured the cross, despising the shame, and is set down at the right hand of the throne of God. For consider him that endured such contradiction of sinners against himself, lest ye be wearied and faint in your minds. If you think you endure injustice and unfairness.

Jesus sacrificed Himself for the very ones who killed Him. In their evilness, they killed Him and through His death, His murderers were given a path to salvation. . . Ye have not yet resisted unto blood, striving against sin. 5 And ye have forgotten the exhortation which speaketh unto you as unto children, my son, despise not thou the chastening of the Lord, nor faint when thou art rebuked of him: For whom the Lord loveth he chasteneth, and scourgeth every son whom he receiveth. If ye endure chastening, God dealeth with you as with sons; for what son is he whom the father chasteneth not? But if ye be without chastisement, whereof all are partakers, then are ye bastards, and not sons.

Furthermore we have had fathers of our flesh which corrected us, and we gave them reverence: shall we not much rather be in subjection unto the Father of spirits, and live? For they verily for a few days chastened us after their own pleasure; but he for our profit, that we might be partakers of his holiness. Now no chastening for the present seemeth to be joyous, but grievous: nevertheless, afterward it yieldeth the peaceable fruit of righteousness unto them which are exercised thereby. Wherefore lift up the hands which hang down, and the feeble knees; And make straight paths for your feet, lest that which is lame be turned out of the way; but let it rather be healed. Follow peace with all men, and holiness, without which no man shall see the Lord:

Looking diligently lest any man fail of the grace of God; lest any root of bitterness springing up trouble you, and thereby many be defiled. (Hebrews 12:1–15)

We do not enjoy our chastisement from God, but if we endure it with an agreeable heart, it will bring forth righteousness in us. Our reaction to His correction determines its result. If we reject His correction, we deny His right as a Father and thereby deny Him.

26. Jehovah Sel'ix—The Lord My Rock

The LORD is my rock, and my fortress, and my deliverer; my God, my strength, in whom I will trust; my buckler, and the horn of my salvation, and my high tower. (Psalm 18:2)

The word *rock* appears fifty-seven times in the King James Version.

And the LORD spoke unto Moses, saying, Take the rod, and gather thou the assembly together, thou, and Aaron thy brother, and speak ye unto the rock before their eyes; and it shall give forth his water, and thou shalt bring forth to them water out of the rock: so, thou shalt give the congregation and their beasts drink. And Moses took the rod from before the LORD, as he commanded him. And Moses and Aaron gathered the congregation together before the rock, and he said unto them, hear now, ye rebels; must we fetch you water out of this rock? And Moses lifted up his hand, and with his rod he smote the rock twice: and the water came out abundantly, and the congregation drank, and their beasts also. And the LORD spoke unto Moses and Aaron, because ye believed me not, to sanctify me in the eyes of the children of Israel, therefore ye shall not bring this congregation into the land which I have given them. (Numbers 20:7–12)

Moreover, brethren, I would not that ye should be ignorant, how that all our fathers were under the cloud, and all passed through the sea; And were all baptized unto Moses in the cloud and in the sea; And did all eat the same spiritual meat; And did all drink the same spiritual drink: for they drank of that spiritual Rock that followed them: and that Rock was Christ. (1 Corinthians 10:1–4)

The rock of God is the solid foundation on which my salvation rests. Only the foolish man built on sand; we must be wise and build on solid rock.

The Eagle and the Rock

When an eagle learn to fly, it will find a rock, claim it, and keep it as its forever. Why do some Christians claim a rock but leave it in times of trouble? David said, "Wait upon the Lord, my soul wait only upon him, for my expectations is from God, for He only is my rock." (Psalms 62:5).

If we start on the Rock, we need to end up on the Rock. If we start with Jesus Christ, we need to end up with Jesus Christ. Nothing else will work out. I stand on Christ, the solid Rock. All other ground is sinking sand.

An Eagle That Gets Away from Its Rock

An eagle that gets away from its rock will become weak, and while it's dying, it will look toward that rock. It will remember how it once flew and was majestic, and it will wish it were back on its rock.

Some remember the highs they once had in the Lord, their mountaintop experiences when they walked with the Lord. But they got away from the Rock. Something happened, and they are no longer soaring. They have drifted away from that Rock. If you get back to your Rock, Jesus will still be there.

A strong eagle will die on its rock with its wings folded in sweet repose and its eyes lifted toward heaven. When I die, I don't want to die away from God. I want to go standing on the Rock of my salvation with my eyes toward heaven. I'm determined to stay on that Rock.

Some of us have come real close to walking away from God. What would they go back to? Lot and his family left Sodom; they could have turned around if they wanted to (his wife did). What was back there? Nothing but ashes.

You may find a club, go back to drugs and alcohol, but there's coming a day when that club will be an ash heap. There's pleasure in sin for a season. The eagle found out that when it got away from the rock, it weakened and died.

The Moping Period

An eagle will go through a moping period. It leaves its rock for the wilderness and walks around like a chicken. It enjoys the look and feel of the wilderness and stays there. But when it gets ready to leave, it discovers it can no longer fly.

I asked my Indian guide why eagles go through a moping period. He said because they abandoned the God-given place and God-given ability of their lives. God never ordained that an eagle should walk in the wilderness and scratch like a chicken.

Christians are walking with their heads dropped because they no longer have the intimacy of locking hands with God and reaching the heights of His glory. The wilderness will destroy you; if you don't believe that, find out what happened to Israel. Because of their unbelief, they wandered in the wilderness for forty years.

Eagles can lose their ability to fly in the wilderness, and their eyes will begin to lose moisture. Strong eagles will weep before their Maker, but moping eagles will have dry eyes; they can no longer weep. When they get down in the wilderness, their heads hang. They no longer look majestic. Their feet swell and bleed. They are in a place God never designed for them. Their talons become dull; they ultimately become just nubs, and they cannot catch prey. Rain, hail, and wind beat on them. They cannot fly above the clouds, above the storms.

We could avoid many storms in life if we stayed where God has put us. Eagles can sense storms coming from a mile away, but when they are moping in the wilderness, they can do nothing about storms.

God Will Take Care of Them

The eagles' feathers are ruffled; they no longer look majestic or honorable. They're dying. But after a while, you hear wings flapping. Other eagles are dropping fresh meat to those moping eagles, and it's up to the eagles to eat, gain strength, and get back to their rocks.

After those eagles drop the meat, they fly around and start making noise. They become cheerleaders and encourage the weak eagles to eat the meat so they can get out of the valley.

Some of you right now need to get back to that Rock. It may not be easy, but it's the only way. There is nothing more refreshing than to get back to the place of fellowship with God, feel refreshed and renovated, and be able to weep before our Maker.

Eagles that make it out of the wilderness will never go there again, but they may fly over the wilderness to drop a rabbit or squirrel down to eagles moping there. They're saying, "I've been there and got out. So can you."

Tangen

My Indian guide named this eagle Tangen. We went down to the valley and saw eagles bringing food and dropping it down. My Indian guide said to me, "It's time to go back to the top. There's something I want you to see. Tangen's prayer time."

I asked, "Who is Tangen?"

He said, "Tangen is an eagle who went through the moping period but has made it back to its rock." I asked, "How do you know it's Tangen? There are over twenty eagles up there." He said, "I know where his rock is."

We got to the top of that mountain, and he handed a telescope to me. He told me to zero in on one eagle on a Rock. For fifteen minutes, big tears came out of that eagle's eyes as it looked toward heaven.

Blessed be the Rock! You don't have to die in the wilderness; get back to your Rock!

> The Lord is my Rock, and my Fortress, and my Strength, in whom I will trust. (Psalm 18:2)

> For who is God save the Lord? Or who is a Rock save our God? It is God that girded me with strength, and maketh my way perfect. He maketh my feet like hind's feet, and setteth me upon high places. (Psalm 18:31–33)

> The Lord liveth; and blessed be my Rock; and let the God of my salvation be exalted. (Psalm 18:46)

> For in the time of trouble he shall hide me in His pavilion:
> In the secret of His tabernacle shall He hide me; He shall
> set me upon a Rock. (Psalm 27:5)

> I waited patiently for the Lord; and he inclined unto me
> and heard my cry. He brought me up out of the miry clay,
> and set my feet upon a Rock, and established my goings.
> (Psalm 40:1–2)

There was a time when some of you could carry burdens long distances, but now you're weaker. Some of you have gotten so weak that you say, "God, I can't make it another day. I can't handle another trial." You feel you've lost all your strength. There's a remedy for that. Look to the Rock. Get back to the mountaintop. If you've lost your ability to soar high above the storms, get back to your Rock. If you're going through the moping period and storms are beating on you, eat, regain your strength, and get back to your Rock.

Peter the Rock

I want to talk about Peter, who was living his life the way he thought he should until Jesus stepped into his life.

> When Simon Peter saw it [a miracle], he fell down at
> Jesus knees, saying, depart from me; for I am a sinful
> man. (Luke 5:8)

Peter was saying, "I am devoted to sin. I am loyal to sin. I am committed to sin. I am faithful to sin." Why are some of us still loyal to sin? Some of us spend more time with our sin than we do with our kids. If you haven't come to hate pornography, you're committed to it more than you are your family. You in essence are saying, "I love this sin more than I do my wife and kids. I don't love them enough to protect them from this junk."

We choose to live below the standard God has set for us because like Simon, we've become less than we should be. If we don't think we can ever be holy as He is, we can never be holy as He is. Did He lie when he said that? Did He say something He thought he could not accomplish? So when we think negatively, we will live negatively toward God.

I believe that Simon was saying more than "Get away from me, for I am devoted to sin." I believe Simon was speaking about more than his actions. I think he was speaking how he saw himself. The name Simon means "Broken Reed." *Broken* means "reduced to fragments." Do you feel you've been reduced to something you shouldn't be? Has your divorce broken you so badly that you don't even know who you feel like anymore? When that person touched you as a child, did that make you feel less than a human?

Did you grow up in an encouraging household? When I grew up, I had many words spoken over me. Is it hard for you to get all that stuff off you? Does it make you feel insecure? Do you fear failure? Has anybody ever been there? Are you afraid you'll become what they said you would? Thank God there's a grace that will remove these thoughts from your mind so you can become what He has called you to be.

Simon was telling Jesus, "Don't you understand, Jesus, that I'm not functioning as I should be? That my life is broken to pieces? I'm just a fragment of what I should be. I am weak and unreliable. Jesus, you should escape from me because I am nothing like you." Is there anybody who has felt that way before? Did Jesus slam him? Devalue him? Did He need to apologize to him because He must have gotten in the wrong boat? Did He tell him he would never be good enough? No. Here's what Jesus said.

> Jesus said to Simon (the broken reed), "Fear not; from henceforth thou shall catch men." (Luke 5:10)

From now on, you will be a soul winner; from now on, you will be a preacher of righteousness, an apostle who will walk with my authority. Your shadow will heal the sick. Simon, you are like many of my children— you know what is wrong with you, but I'm here to tell you what is right with you. You have a negative image of yourself that makes you unaware of the greatness I have placed inside you. The Bible says God swoops down and make you great.

Simon, I know all you can see is dirt, but I see gold in you. You see junk, but I see value. I know you see a messed-up life, but I see a life worth dying for. You see someone who is unreliable, but I see you have a divine purpose. I know who you can be.

We have something in common with Simon—a big distance between who we are and who we are called to be.

> For I know the thoughts that I think toward you, says the Lord, thoughts of peace and not of evil, to give you a future and hope. (Jeremiah 29:11 NKJV)

> Your eyes saw my substance, being yet unformed. And in your book, they were written, the days fashioned for me, when as yet there were none of them. (Psalm 139:16 NKJV)

God knows all the days of your life. He knows where He is trying to get you. He knows your destiny.

Peter means "rock." A rock is solid, strong, stable, not easily moved or broken unlike a reed. It's like Christ. We were taken from the mire and placed on a rock—everything we are with Jesus. It is everything we are not when we are not with Him. So Jesus is saying, "Simon, I know when you look at yourself, all you can see is a broken reed, but I see you different from the way you see yourself." Are you not glad that He sees us differently than we see ourselves?

But even after Jesus said that, Peter did not live that way at first. He messed up. He made mistakes. Sometimes, he acted like Peter, but other times, he acted like Simon. Sometimes, he was solid, but other times, he was weak.

We can learn a lot about the heart of God in our Simon Peter moments. In Mark 14:37, Jesus went to the Garden of Gethsemane. His soul was in anguish. He was about to go to the cross. He took James, John, and Peter with Him for prayer support. Then this happens in verse 37: "And He cometh, and findeth them sleeping, and saith unto to (the rock) Peter, (broken reed) Simon, 'Sleepest thou? You're acting like a broken reed when you have been called a rock? Couldest not thou watch one hour? Watch ye and pray, lest ye enter into temptation.'" That was a Simon moment.

> And the Lord said Simon, Simon, (broken reed, broken reed) behold, Satan hath desired to have you, that he may sift you as wheat. But I have prayed for you,(Why? because I believe in you) that thy faith fail not: and when thou art converted, strengthen thy brethren. (Luke 22:31–32)

I know at times you'll fall flat on your face, be a broken reed, have a Simon moment. But when you come back to your senses and remember you've been called to be a rock, I ask you to strengthen the brethren.

> And he said, I tell thee, Peter, (he is reminding him who he has called to be) the cock shall not crow this day, before that thou shalt thrice deny that thou knowest me. (Luke 22:34)

When Jesus was arrested, Peter acted like a Simon, a broken reed. He followed the mob that had arrested Jesus at a distance. Whenever you follow Jesus at a distance, the outcome will never be good. It is an intimacy that allows you to live a holy life and walk in the expectation He wants you to walk in.

Peter is found comfortably standing by a fire. Out of fear, he denied Jesus twice and then a third time to a girl. How did he convince her he didn't walk with Jesus? The Bible says he cussed. So listen, cussing saints, next time you're saying whatever you want to say, remember those people who are around you, and remember you're called to be a witness to the Son of God. Don't cuss; that tells others you don't walk with Him.

Simon, the broken reed, denied Jesus three times. I believe everyone who is reading this is thankful that God is the God of second chances, third chances, fourth chances, and more. The Bible tells us that this confused, broken reed, solid rock, Simon Peter, was saved, was baptized in the Holy Spirit, preached like a man on fire, and saved 3,000.

That's Acts 2. Go to Acts 4; it talks about John the beloved. He is walking with John one day to the temple for prayer, and they come by a crippled person sitting at the gate and asking for spare change. I love that; it shows Peter being the rock. Where does this preaching of the gospel land Peter and John? In prison!

> And it came to pass on the next day, that their rulers, elders, and scribes, as well as Annas the High Priest, Caiaphas (remember his name). John, and Alexander, and as many as were of the family of the High Priest, were gathered together at Jerusalem. (Acts 4:5–7 NKJV)

So they're put in prison, and the religious folk decide to mess with Peter and John. They are brought before these religious people. And when they had set them in their midst, they asked, "By what power or by what name have you done this?"

The last time, Peter denied Christ three times. I can imagine John being the only one who did not flee the garden. Peter followed at a distance. John was the only one to die a natural death; maybe God honored his faithfulness that way. So Peter the Rock is sitting by the beloved, the one who's always right. They ask by what name has he done this. Peter looks to John and says, "Quiet please. It's my time to do this. God has given me a second chance." Does anybody need a second chance? Look at verses 8–12.

> Then Peter (Rock), filled with the Holy Spirit, said to them, rulers of the people and elders of Israel: If we this day are judged for a good deed done to a helpless man, by which means he has been made well. Let it be known to you all, and to the people of Israel, that by the Name of Jesus Christ of Nazareth, whom you crucified, whom God raised from the dead, by him this man stands before you whole. This is the stone that was rejected by you builders, which has become the chief cornerstone. Nor is there salvation in any other, for there is no other name

under Heaven given unto men by which we must be saved.

Now read verses 13–14.

Now when they saw the Boldness of Peter (the Rock) and John, and perceived that they were uneducated and untrained men, they marveled. And they realized that they had been with Jesus. (No longer following at a distance). And seeing the man who had been healed standing with them, they could not say nothing against it.

The lion inside him is not breakable. He let the lion of Judah that is in every one of us come out. God is not a little kitty cat; He is a Lion longing to come out of you.

Let me show you the coolest part of this scripture. Who was the high priest Jesus stood in front of and Peter denied himself? Caiaphas! Caiaphas means, "The Rooster Is Crowing Again!"

27. Jehovah Eli—Lord My God

> The LORD is my rock, and my fortress, and my deliverer;
> my God, my strength, in whom I will trust; my buckler,
> and the horn of my salvation, and my high tower. (Psalm
> 18:2)

The Lord is my rock, my fortress and my deliverer; my God is my rock
in whom I take refuge. He is my shield and the horn of my salvation, my
stronghold. Lord is His relationship to us. Godship is what He is.

> Look unto me, and be ye saved, all the ends of the earth: for
> I am God, and there is none else. I have sworn by myself,
> the word is gone out of my mouth in righteousness, and
> shall not return, that unto me every knee shall bow, every
> tongue shall swear. (Isaiah 45:22–23)

My Lord and My God

Jesus Christ is God, and Jesus Christ is Lord! We don't make Him
Lord by calling Him Lord. We recognize His lordship and submit to His
lordship when we make Him our Lord.

> For ye are bought with a price: therefore, glorify God in
> your body, and in your spirit, which are God's. He owns
> you! He purchased you at the high cost of His blood! (1
> Corinthians 6:20)

> Which is the earnest of our inheritance until the
> redemption of the purchased possession, until the praise
> of His Glory. (Ephesians 1:14)

For this reason alone, He deserves to be recognized as your Lord. He wants to be your Lord because He loves you and came to save you from sin and hell.

God gave us His Son; He has a lot invested in us, so He will take care of us. His resurrection proves He is Lord, and His resurrection is more reason He deserves to be Lord of our lives. Every living creature, whether in heaven (angels), hell (lost), or on earth will one day proclaim Him Lord.

28. Jehovah Elyon—The Lord God Most High

In Genesis 14:19, God is the Most High and possessor of heaven and earth. "Blessed be Abram of the most high God, possessor of heaven and earth." He owns the universe. He can control every situation in our lives.

> Blessed be the most-high God, which hath delivered thine enemies into thine hand. (Genesis 14:20)

God will deliver your enemies into your hands. When you consider that Abram had 318 servants to fight the armies of the mightiest nations of that day, you realize how great Abram's God had to have been. Claim God's promise to be Jehovah Elyon in your life; say, "I am delivered."

The Lord Most High Is Terrible

> They shalt not be affrighted at them: for the Lord thy God is among you, a MIGHTY GOD AND TERRIBLE. And the Lord thy God will put out those nations before thee by little and little: Thou mayest not consume them at once, lest the beasts of the field increase upon thee. But the Lord thy God SHALL DELIVER THEM UNTO THEE, AND SHALL DESTROY THEM WITH A MIGHTY DESTRUCTION, until they are destroyed. And he shall deliver their Kings into thine hand, and thou shalt destroy their name from under Heaven: There shall NO MAN BE ABLE TO STAND BEFORE THEE, until thou hast destroyed them. (Deuteronomy 7:21–24)

David

Several kingdoms could tell you that the most high Lord is terrible. The Philistines would tell you how a young boy, David, put an army to flight.

Meaning of the Lord Most High Is Terrible

It is believed that when the children of Israel built a house of worship, they did so on the highest hill they could so it would be visible to all. They believed God to be the Lord Most High. They believed God to be in their midst. They believed the God of Abraham, Isaac, and Jacob walked with them and talked with them.

He was not *a* god; He was *the* God, the *only* God. God told Moses, "I Am," which means ever present. In Exodus, we read that God chose the children of Israel because they had chosen this most high God: They didn't choose the god of the Nile; they chose a God who was above the sun, who held the universe in His hands. Who formed the stars with His fingers. Who spoke the world into existence. This is the one I am talking about; the Lord Most High is terrible.

> God is our refuge and strength, a very present help in trouble. Therefore, will not we fear, though the earth be removed, and though the mountains be carried into the midst of the sea; Though the waters therefore roar and be troubled, though the mountains shake with the swelling thereof: Selah. There is a river, the streams whereof shall make glad the City of God, the Holy Place of the Tabernacles of THE MOST-HIGH. God is in the midst of her; she shall not be moved: God shall help her, and that right early. The heathen raged, and Kingdoms were moved: He uttered His voice and the earth melted. The Lord of Host is with us (God of the Battles), the God of Jacob is our refuge. Selah.

> Come, behold the works of the Lord, what desolations He has made in the earth, He makes wars to cease unto the end of the earth: He breaks the bow, and cuts the spear in sunder: He burns the chariots in the fire. Be still, and know that I am God: I will be exalted among the heathen, I will be exalted in the earth. The Lord of

Hosts is with us; the God of Jacob is our refuge. Selah.
(Psalm 46:1–11)

Psalm 46 puts this in perspective. God's house was built in Jerusalem. The word *Jerusalem* in Hebrew means "peace." The city was founded on peace. God put His house in the highest place and built it on the foundation of peace. God's house is to be a place with a name above reproach, a beacon, a light on the hill. He is high and lifted up. He said, "My ways are not your ways, my thoughts are not your thoughts. I am above anything you can imagine."

Verse 1 tells us that God is our refuge, the One to run to in times of trouble. David said, "Hide me in that Rock that is higher than I." A place that we can be hidden away, where Satan cannot find us. Job said, "Hide me in the grave until all of this be passed." Even in the grave, I am protected. I am telling you there's nowhere to run or hide except in God. He is our refuge, our bomb shelter in times of trouble. He is our refuge and our strength.

Verse 5 reads, "God is in the midst of her." This puts it in the right perspective of the Lord being the Most High. The children of Israel believed this; I wonder if we do. David was saying that God stood in our midst. Jesus told His disciples, "I'll never leave you or forsake you"; He is in our midst. Jesus said, "Whenever two or three are gathered in my name, there I'll be in their midst." God is in the midst of His church where two or more are gathered in His name.

To know verse 5 is to read the other verses of Psalm 46 and never be shaken.

THOU the earth be removed, God is in the midst of her. THOU the mountains be carried into the midst of the sea; God is in the midst of her. THOU the waters should roar and be troubled, know that God is in the midst of her. THOU the mountains shake with the swellings thereof, know that God is in the midst of her.

We wonder how people can take what they go through sometimes. The devil is more than a match for us, but God comes down to be in our midst and stand with us in battle.

In verse 6, we read, "The heathen raged, but God is in the midst of her." We see communism as it once tried to engulf this world. Seventy percent of the world's people are under its fist. Why do they have to put up steel walls and iron curtains? Because they're afraid of what America has in its midst—God. They know that if they would let up for just a short time, people would pour out of China in a flood. They're having revivals in Russia; God is moving across the land. God's Word is being preached in China; the truth keeps marching on. The devil is trying to put up steel walls, but God is in the midst of China; He's all over the world.

Verse 6 reads, "God uttered His voice and the earth melted." He just spoke. If God just tilted this earth just slightly, huge waves 500 feet or more would engulf the earth. God's not afraid of the mess that's going on in the world today; He said He would destroy it at the brightness of His coming. He will throw that bunch—the devil, the beast, and the false prophet—into the lake of fire where they will be tormented forever.

Job

Job thought he could stump God if he asked God enough questions. But as he asked questions, that whirlwind moved closer and closer to him. "Who is this (God speaking) that darkens its counsel without words of knowledge (Who's this fool talking?), who asks questions and doesn't even know what he's asking?" How many times have we blamed God and acted as if He didn't know what He was doing? Some of us act as if God doesn't have any sense. But His ways are above ours.

Scientists tell us it's impossible for a bumblebee to fly, but God works His wonders. "Is there anything too hard for the Lord?" He hung the world on nothing. We worry, but God takes care of everything. He's in our midst, but we don't act as if He is. We don't realize God will take care of us. The Bible says, "The steps of a righteous man are ordered by the Lord."

We often don't understand why things happen to us, but sometimes, God is taking us to school. It may be the school of hard knocks, but when we graduate, we'll be able to pass any tests down the road.

Job heard, "Get up now on thine loins like a man. Since you have so many questions, I have some for you." Some of us act as if because we graduated from high school and have our little degrees, we can act as if nobody can tell us what to do. "Where were you when I laid the foundations of the earth?" I want to ask scientists, "Which one of you saw the big bang? Where were you when this world came together?"

"Who hath laid the measure thereof?" Who measured this thing? Who got it within 24,000 miles in circumference and made the diameter the thickness that it was? Who got the sun far enough away? Who measured it? When you can put 93 million earths inside the sun 93 million miles away, it's closer to the earth in the winter than in the summer, but why is it colder?

Can you tell me who did the measuring? Who laid the cornerstone? You have to have somewhere to stand when you lay a foundation. God was asking who was standing where when He created earth. He hung this world on nothing. The morning stars sang, and all the sons of God shouted for joy.

Just like a clock, the tide goes in and out. Who made that happen? Job, answer me. Tell me. I made the clouds the garments that hold water and move it from California to North Carolina without a drop falling. Job, have you ever entered the spring of the sea and walked to its depths?

He said there was coming a time when He would break the high minded, the proud, the sinner, and the wicked. The Bible says Job covered his mouth. Some of us need to do that sometimes—stop asking questions and believe that what He's done for others He'll do for you. Some of us need to wake up and realize God is in our midst. Stop shaking and running every time the devil attacks you like an elevator going up and down spiritually.

29. Adonai—The Lord God

> And Abram said, Lord GOD, what wilt thou give me,
> seeing I go childless, and the steward of my house is this
> Eliezer of Damascus?" And Abram said, Behold, to me
> thou hast given no seed: and, lo, one born in my house
> is mine heir. And, behold, the word of the LORD came
> unto him, saying, this shall not be thine heir; but he that
> shall come forth out of thine own bowels shall be thine
> heir. And he brought him forth abroad, and said, look
> now toward heaven, and tell the stars, if thou be able to
> number them: and he said unto him, so shall thy seed be.
> And he believed in the LORD; and he counted it to him
> for righteousness. (Genesis 15:2–6)

The name Adonai challenges everyone who calls God Lord to live in a way
that demonstrates His lordship. "He is Lord" must be not only with our
lips but also with our life! A dangerous deception is to call Him "Lord,
Lord" but refuse to submit to Him in loving obedience. The name Adonai
speaks of obedience as servants would obey their masters.

> Many will say to Me in that day, Lord, Lord have we not
> prophesy in Your name, cast out demons in your name,
> and done many wonders in Your name, and then I will
> declare to them, I never knew you; DEPART FROM ME,
> YOU WHO PRACTICE LAWLESSNESS. (Matthew
> 7:23 NKJV)

Every knee will bow to acknowledge Jesus Christ as Lord. God has
exalted Him above all so all will submit to Jesus as Lord. Jesus did not
exalt Himself; the Father put His stamp of approval on Jesus's death as the
satisfaction of the penalty for our sins. But people did not exalt Jesus; they
jeered Him and spat on Him. But the Father gave Jesus the name above
all names, the name Lord, which is equivalent to the Old Testament name

of God. When they were reading the scripture, and came to Yahweh, they would read, "Adonai," which means "Lord." "Jesus is Lord" means "Jesus is Yahweh," eternal God.

Public schools may ban Him and outlaw prayer, but they can't change His reality. The media may deny His existence, yet the truth remains. When He comes again, He will deal with the ungodly sinners who have spoken against Him. Many are laughing now, but they won't when they face His justice. "Vengeance is Mine, I will repay," says the Lord.

May we be so surrendered to Jesus that like David, we cry out, "You are my Adonai. I have no god besides you."

30. Jehovah-Adon Kal Ha'arets— The Lord of All the Earth

> And it shall come to pass, as soon as the soles of the feet of the priests that bear the ark of the LORD, the Lord of all the earth, shall rest in the waters of Jordan, that the waters of Jordan shall be cut off from the waters that come down from above; and they shall stand upon a heap. (Joshua 3:13)

God is ruler of not just political entities or people but of all the earth. What human ruler can make a fleece damp one night dry the next let alone put a rainbow in the sky as a sign, cause it to rain for forty days and forty nights, or withhold rain for three years? The sun stood still and the moon stayed until the people had avenged themselves on their enemies.

Our God provides for each of us, knows each of us by name, knows the number of the hairs on our heads, knows us even before we are in our mothers' wombs. He loves us more than anyone else; He loves us even when we aren't loveable.

We worship the triune God, the Creator and Lord of all things.

> For since the creation of the world His invisible attributes are clearly seen, being understood by the things that are made, even His eternal power and Godhead, so that they are without excuse. (Romans 1:20 NKJV)

Only a fool would say in his heart, "There is no God." On a clear night with no city lights, we can see as many as 6,000 stars and planets with the naked eye. The deepest spot in the ocean is over a mile deeper than the tallest mountain. Thirteen thousand, three hundred kinds of fish exist. Scientists have described and named about a million kinds of animals. Of these, more than 800,000 are insects. The human heart beats 100,000 times a day through arteries and vessels that would stretch 60,000 miles. The ball in our heads that we call a brain contains 10 to 100 billion neurons linked in amazing complexity to smoothly control our five senses. As we look at the world around us, how can we do anything but bow to the Lord of all earth?

Lord of Jew and Gentile

The Word says Israel is a chosen generation and you are a chosen generation. Israel is a royal priesthood and a holy nation, and so are you. Israel is a particular treasure, and you are a particular people. Israel is the wife of Jehovah; you are the bride of Christ. Israel builds the temple; you *are* the temple. Israel is given a law; you are given a law. Israel's law is a physical law; yours is a spiritual law.

Israel's law was given on Mount Sinai; your law was given on Mount Zion. Israel's law is the Ten Commandments; your law is the law of spirit and life. The same day Israel was given the Law in the Old Testament, Pentecost took place and the Holy Spirit descended. When the Law was given, there was thundering and lightning; when the Holy Spirit came, there was fire and wind. That law was on a table of stones, this law is on the table of your heart. That law was written with the finger of God; this law was written by the Spirit of God. When that law was given, 3,000 people died; when this law was given, 3,000 people lived. They were given a covenant; you are given a covenant: the Abrahamic covenant in Genesis 12, the Davidic Covenant in 2 Samuel 7, and the land covenants in Deuteronomy. You were given the new covenant. Their covenant is built on the blood of bulls, goats, turtledoves, pigeons, and lambs; your covenant is built on the precious blood of Jesus Christ.

If God raised, preserved, defended, blessed, and increased Israel for animal blood, how much more will he bless you with better blood, priests, law, and covenant?

31. Jehovah Bara—The Lord Creator

> Hast thou not known? hast thou not heard, that the
> everlasting God, the LORD, the Creator of the ends
> of the earth, fainteth not, neither is weary? there is no
> searching of his understanding. (Isaiah 40:28)

There are two words in the Hebrew language that translate as "create" in English. One means to create out of existing materials while the other means to create out of nothing. It's *bara*, the second, that's joined with the name of God to form the name Jehovah-Bara.

God can make something out of nothing. At best, we can create things from materials. We see bara in action when He spoke the universe into existence (Hebrews 11:3). We also see it at the end of time when He creates a new heaven and a new earth (Isaiah 65:17).

The New Jerusalem

John said,

> I was in the spirit on the Lord's day, while on the Island of
> Patmos, I had a Revelation of Jesus Christ. He appeared
> unto me and shared some things with me. He said you
> write down the things I tell you about now and the things
> that are going to be.

John says that city's foundations were made by God. John said it was amazing; its walls were as jasper, it had twelve gates made of pearl, and each gate was a single pearl. He said this city had twelve foundations all made of different precious stones. He said that city was as glimmering solid gold. He said the streets were like gold and transparent as glass. "I looked and saw a throne of God, there out of the throne of God flows a crystal river called the river of life. It flows out of the throne of God and it flowed all around the regions thereof." Trees on the banks of this river, trees of life, bore different kinds of fruit every month.

The leaves on the trees were for the healing of the nations. There was no sun or moon there because the glory of God was the light of the city and the lamb was the lamp thereof. He said there was no night there because the glory of God totally illuminated the place, and people were able to go in and out of the city. This is what awaits the righteous.

John said that thine eyes shall see the King in His beauty. Thank God for the glory and beauty of heaven, but thank Him most for our risen Lord who loved us and gave His life for us.

Elijah

> But he himself went a day's journey into the wilderness, and came and sat down under a juniper tree: and he requested for himself that he might die; and said, it is enough; now, O LORD, take away my life; for I am not better than my fathers. (1 Kings 19:4)

Elijah had his huge victory over the prophets of Baal in chapter 18. You would think that display of God's power would have been enough to sustain Elijah for the rest of his life. But Jezebel sends a message to Elijah that she's hunting for him to take his life, and Elijah is ready to give up. Elijah forgot. How often do we forget just a short time after God has brought victory into our lives? He is the everlasting Creator of all.

32. Jehovah Hamelech—The Lord the King

O sing unto the LORD a new song; for he hath done marvelous things: his right hand, and his holy arm, hath gotten him the victory. The LORD hath made known his salvation: his righteousness hath he openly showed in the sight of the heathen. He hath remembered his mercy and his truth toward the house of Israel: all the ends of the earth have seen the salvation of our God. Make a joyful noise unto the LORD, all the earth: make a loud noise, and rejoice, and sing praise. Sing unto the LORD with the harp; with the harp, and the voice of a psalm. With trumpets and sound of cornet make a joyful noise before the LORD, the King. Let the sea roar, and the fullness thereof; the world, and they that dwell therein. Let the floods clap their hands: let the hills be joyful together Before the LORD; for he cometh to judge the earth: with righteousness, shall he judge the world, and the people with equity. (Psalm 98:1–9)

There are references, prophecies for the future.

Rejoice greatly, O daughter of Zion; shout, O daughter of Jerusalem: behold, thy King cometh unto thee: he is just, and having salvation; lowly, and riding upon an ass, and upon a colt the foal of an ass. (Zechariah 9:9)

Tell ye the daughter of Zion, Behold, thy king cometh unto thee, meek, and sitting upon an ass, and a colt the foal of an ass. (Matthew 21:5)

There is not a single verse in which God declares Himself King. The closest He comes to that was when He was being interviewed by Pilate: "And Jesus stood before the governor: and the governor asked him, saying, Art thou the King of the Jews? And Jesus said unto him, Thou sayest" (Matthew 27:11). That would have been a good time for Jesus to speak. I've wondered why Jesus did not proclaim Himself then. I think maybe the same principle was in operation here. If God were to loudly proclaimed His kingship, that would weaken His status. Our president doesn't go around telling everyone he's the president; that would display insecurity.

33. Jehovah Melech 'Olam— The Lord King Forever

> The LORD is King forever and ever: the heathen are perished out of his land. (Psalm 10:16)

God Is Self-Existent

His life is in Himself. The Hebrews called Him Jehovah—One who exists of Himself and who gives being and existence to others. God has no beginning or end.

God Is Spirit

As Spirit, He is invisible to the human eye. "Now to the King eternal, immortal, invisible, to God who alone is wise, be honor and glory forever and ever, Amen" (1 Timothy 1:17 NKJV).

God is not subject to the limitations of a physical body; He is eternal: "Before the mountains were brought forth, or ever You had formed the earth and the world, even from everlasting to everlasting, you are God" (Psalm 90:2).

He is "from everlasting to everlasting," neither beginning nor ending. God is immutable: "For I am the LORD, I do not change; Therefore, you are not consumed, O sons of Jacob" (Malachi 3:6 NKJV). God does not change; He is not like us, who grow weaker and older. His character, truth, and ways never change.

God Is Omnipotent

> And I heard, as it were, the voice of a great multitude, as the sound of many waters and as the sound of mighty thundering's, saying, "Alleluia! For the Lord God, Omnipotent reigns!" (Revelation 19:6)

God's unlimited power is being joyfully proclaimed by those who stand before Him in eternity.

God is Omniscient

He knows all things.

> Knowing that you were not redeemed with corruptible things, like silver or gold, from your aimless conduct received by tradition from your fathers, 19 but with the precious blood of Christ, as of a lamb without blemish and without spot. 20 He indeed was foreordained before the foundation of the world, but was manifest in these last times for you. (Peter 1:18–20 NKJV)

God knows past, present, and future. He knew we would fall, so he predestined our reconciliation through Jesus Christ.

God Declares the End from the Beginning

We start from the beginning; God starts from the end. He never works forward; he always acts backward because in His mind, the work is already done. So when the devil tells you you're not going to make it, tell him, "My Father has decided my destiny. So devil, get out of my face." God can turn around to His glory everything the enemy does.

Remember when Lazarus died?

> Now a certain man was sick, Lazarus of Bethany. The town of Mary and her sister Martha. It was that Mary who anointed the Lord with fragrant Oil and Wiped his feet with her hair, whose brother Lazarus was sick. Therefore, the sister sent to Him, saying, "Lord, behold, he whom you love is sick." When Jesus heard that, He said, "This sickness is not unto death, but for the glory of God, that the Son of God may be glorified through it." (John 11:1–4 NKJV)

It's not that the sickness brought glory to God; it's that in the midst of the sickness, God will turn it around and derive glory out of it through Jesus.

The moment that God shows up, things will change. The moment you pray, the moment you declare, the moment you stand, you take ownership because you are in partnership with God. Lazarus has died. Jesus shows up and does something off base with religion and human thinking; it doesn't line up with a hopeless situation. He declares life from the beginning. He declares victory over death. He declares what He will do and see. Jesus tells them to roll the stone away and says, "Lazarus, come out!" He is declaring life in the midst of darkness; He is declaring healing, restoration, and deliverance in the midst of what looks like hopelessness. He declares light in darkness, and light always wins.

Hope declares light to darkness. We gather ourselves, we hear the report, we gather our emotions, we gather our thoughts because of what we see—God's promise of light in darkness. We all experience darkness; it gets in our face. But God said He'd never forsake us. He's right there with us no matter what comes. The Spirit of God is in us always and in every situation.

There is emptiness, there is confusion, but nothing happens until God does something. God is getting ready to declare light in darkness, the end from the beginning. The beginning was darkness; that was all there was. God declared, "Let there be light," and there was light.

Joseph said to his brothers, who had sold him out,

> Do not be afraid, for am I in the place of God. But as for you, you meant evil against me; but God meant it for good, in order to bring it about as it is this day, to save many people alive. (Genesis 50:19–20 NKJV)

"I am in the place of God." That's for somebody right now who means evil against me, but God meant it for good. People may slander you, treat you unjustly, steal from you, and mess things up for you, but I tell you, God is a God of justice. He's got your back; He's got your front; He's got your right side, and He's got your left side. Regardless of who messes with you, they're not more powerful or bigger than God. If He is for us, who can be against us?

Whatever bad people have done to you, God will turn it around for your good, your blessing, and He will receive the glory for that. God does this "to bring it about as it is this day, to save many people alive." God took what people or the devil did and turned it around for good. He will cover you in all this so people can be saved, changed, and full of hope even in hopeless situations.

The devil may bring a pick, a shovel, and a tractor to dig the biggest hole you've ever seen in your life, and he may push you in it, but God will bring you out of the pit, and the devil and everything that was against you will go in that pit, and God will cover it up.

Every time we pray, we give God ownership of our situation; that's why we should pray about everything. I don't give up; I declare to the darkness what that Word says. I declare the end from the beginning.

Remember Joshua at the huge walls of Jericho? God showed up and told Joshua, "See, I have given you the city." That was before they marched and shouted. God wanted Joshua to see the end from the beginning.

God Is Faithful

His Word will never fail.

> Let your conduct be without covetousness; and be content with such things as you have. For He Himself has said, "I will never leave you nor forsake you." (Hebrews 13:5 NKJV)

> Can a woman forget her nursing child, and not have compassion on the son of her womb? Surely, they may forget, yet I will not forget you. (Isaiah 49:15 NKJV)

Could any mother forget to nurse her child? In the same way, God cannot forget Israel. God is forever faithful; that never changes. He is everlasting.

Lord, thou hast been our dwelling place in all generations. Before the mountains were brought forth (brought forth into existence—implies before Creation) or ever thou hadst formed the earth and the world, even from everlasting (Olam) to everlasting (Olam), thou art God (Elohim). (Psalm 90:1–2a)

Now to Him (The Everlasting God) Who is able to keep you from stumbling and to present you faultless before the presence of His glory with exceeding joy, to God our savior, who alone is wise, BE GLORY AND MAJESTY, DOMINION AND POWER, BOTH NOW AND FOREVER AMEN. (Jude 24–25 NKJV)

34. Jehovah Kanna—The Lord Whose Name Is Jealous

> For thou shalt worship no other god: for the LORD, whose name is Jealous, is a jealous God. (Exodus 34:14)

There are only four other verses in which the word *jealous* is used.

> Thou shalt not bow down thyself to them, nor serve them: for I the LORD thy God am a jealous God, visiting the iniquity of the fathers upon the children unto the third and fourth generation of them that hate me. (Exodus 20:5)

> For the LORD thy God is a consuming fire, even a jealous God. (Deuteronomy 4:24)

> Thou shalt not bow down thyself unto them, nor serve them: for I the LORD thy God am a jealous God, visiting the iniquity of the fathers upon the children unto the third and fourth generation of them that hate me. (Deuteronomy 5:9)

> For the LORD thy God is a jealous God among you, lest the anger of the LORD thy God be kindled against thee, and destroy thee from off the face of the earth. (Deuteronomy 6:15)

Humanity has given many other names to God, but I'd give my undivided attention when God gives a name to Himself. There is no mistaking it—our God is a jealous God. God expects our undivided attention and loyalty. My boss expects the same thing. My wife would be a little concerned and hurt, yes even jealous, if I were much worried about making the neighbor woman happy. I don't often treat God as He desires; my whole heart is supposed to be His.

> Thou shalt love the Lord thy God with all thy heart, and
> with all thy soul, and with all thy mind. This is the first
> and great commandment. (Matthew 22:37–38)

He requires us to worship only Him. To worship anything else or any other god is a journey in the wrong direction. He is not a jealous God for His selfish purposes; His love is a place of healing and safety.

Nebuchadnezzar

The king made an idol for everybody to worship; all did what the king wanted them to do except for Shadrack, Meshach, and Abednego. The king was told, "Three young men will not bow down to you or your golden image. They won't run with the crowd; they won't do what the majority is doing. They say they will serve only their God."

The king was enraged. He told them they better bow down, but they said, "O King [they respected him], we are not going to bow down to anybody, and we know you will throw us into that furnace. But we believe our God will deliver us from every affliction and that fiery furnace. Even if He doesn't, we know we have a greater glory and will be standing in the presence of our God and will give him glory, honor, and praise. One way or the other, we will be delivered. We are not going to bow down."

In these last days, there will be people filled with the fire of God and full of conviction. When the enemy comes in like a flood, God will raise up a standard against them. Though in these last days it seems everybody has fallen off the edge, I'm telling you it's dangerous to live on the edge. Just ask Humpty-Dumpty. People are living on the edge trying to find meaning and joy in life, but they won't find it outside Jesus Christ.

They threw the three boys into the fire. The fire was so hot that the men who threw them in were killed. The king walked over and looked down. "Did not we throw three men into the fire? But I see four, and one looks like and is in the image of the Son of God."

No matter what fire you have been thrown into, God is there with you; He will never leave your side. He will not let you burn up and be destroyed.

The king said, "Bring those men out." I believe when they came out they were walking with a little swagger. The king asked, "What happened?" They said, "We told you our God would take care of us." They didn't think twice about it; they didn't compromise on it. They weren't going to bend their knees to the king's idol. They weren't crossing that line. Their lives and convictions were set, sure. They knew what they believed, what they stood for. "Give it your best shot. I serve my God, who will deliver me. Take me down, spit on me, laugh at me, do whatever you want to do to me, but God will bring me back; He will restore me."

Have you ever thought like Nebuchadnezzar? Let me help you to think like him and then I will have you think like God. He said, "Those people are not worshiping my idol, my image." Nebuchadnezzar had built an image so the children of Israel could worship him. Any image that the enemy builds is an image to replace the image of God—it's artificial worship. Worship of the one, true God is the biggest threat to the devil. The devil wants worship. That's why his temptation of Jesus in the wilderness is so important to you. In the wilderness, Jesus said He would not bow to the devil. He wounded the devil with that. From Genesis to Malachi, every prince, king, judge, and priest bowed to the weakness of the flesh. But when the devil came to Jesus, he found He was one man who would not give him worship.

When we worship God, we weaken the enemy; we wound him forever. That's why we strive for worship in church. We don't let people just stare at us; we make them worshipers.

Nebuchadnezzar ordered that the heat be turned up seven times hotter and ordered guards to throw the three into the furnace. Have you ever felt like guards were about to throw you into a very hot furnace? Let me tell you what God was thinking: "Nebuchadnezzar is about to go mad. I need some of my children in power, but to get them in power, I need some of them to go through a furnace so Nebuchadnezzar can see that my power is greater."

So one had a plan to kill and the other had a plan to promote. But it had to be done so that the devil would think he was in control. God does not create trials, or send trials, or plan trials, but He permits trials. God does not create your furnace; the devil does, but God just steps in it, the devil loses his claim over the furnace, and the purpose changes from Nebuchadnezzar's to God's. Whatever furnace you're in, your Father will step in, overturn the devil's plans, and replace them with His. Whatever anyone is going through at the hands of others, God will step in, change it, and bring something miraculous out of it. Out of that furnace, those men became governors in Babylon. They ended up possessing what had possessed them. Babylon had possessed them, but they ended up possessing Babylon. Shout "Hallelujah!" for that right now.

Do you know what the words Shadrack, Meshach, and Abednego means in Hebrew? Shadrack means "attend a field or harvest a field." Meshach means "he who draws with force." Abednego means "servant of light." God is saying he will give you a harvest field, anoint you to draw others with force, and make you a servant of light. Shadrack, Meshach, and Abednego represent your harvest in a fire that is ready to come out.

Do you feel your stuff is in a fire? Do you need God to step into a situation right now? The thing that defines your situation will not define it after God gets into it because you're not defined by what you have gone through; you're defined by what Jesus has gone through.

"I need God to step into a situation for me." Do you need God to step into a furnace for you? How many of you has the enemy tried to disorient and discourage? Worship doesn't exclude you from the furnace; you could be in the furnace even because of your worship. The devil created your furnace to hurt you, but God will step in and promote you. You may want resurrection, but you don't want the cross and the nails and especially not the grave.

I believe God is about to change the fiery furnace for someone in a furnace. I promise that person that no purpose or plan of the enemy will be accomplished in his or her life. I believe promotion is coming to us all in church, at work—wherever we are. God is the God of exaltation coming to you in the name of Jesus, so lift your hands and worship the Lord now.

Lord, bring them out. Father, bring them out of that furnace and release them. Say this with me: "I will not let the length of my waiting or the intensity of my trial rob me of my right to believe that my breakthrough is here right now. Almighty God has stepped into my furnace, my situation, my life, and God is bringing me a harvest."

The three became governors in Babylon while King Nebuchadnezzar ate grass for seven years. God doesn't do that every time, but He has the power to. If your vision isn't bigger than yourself, it didn't come from God.

35. Jehovah Keren-Yish'i—The Lord the Horn of My Salvation

> To the chief Musician, A Psalm of David, the servant of the LORD, who spoke unto the LORD the words of this song in the day that the LORD delivered him from the hand of all his enemies, and from the hand of Saul: And he said, I will love thee, O LORD, my strength. The LORD is my rock, and my fortress, and my deliverer; my God, my strength, in whom I will trust; my buckler, and the horn of my salvation, and my high tower. I will call upon the LORD, who is worthy to be praised: so, shall I be saved from mine enemies. The sorrows of death compassed me, and the floods of ungodly men made me afraid. The sorrows of hell compassed me about: the snares of death prevented me. In my distress, I called upon the LORD, and cried unto my God: he heard my voice out of his temple, and my cry came before him, even into his ears. (Psalm 18:1–6)

A horn of salvation is a source of might. The kind of horn meant here is not a musical instrument but the deadly weapon of war.

> And he said, The LORD is my rock, and my fortress, and my deliverer; The God of my rock; in him will I trust: he is my shield, and the horn of my salvation, my high tower, and my refuge, my savior; thou savest me from violence. I will call on the LORD, who is worthy to be praised: so shall I be saved from mine enemies. (2 Samuel 22:2–4)

> For lo, thy enemies, O Lord, for lo, thy enemies shall perish; all evildoers shall be scattered. But thou hast exalted my horn like that of the wild ox. (Psalm 92:9–10)

The horn is a sign of strength that leads to victory. God said concerning Jerusalem, "There will I make the horn of David to bud: I have ordained a lamp for mine anointed. His enemies will I clothe with shame: but upon himself shall his crown flourish" (Psalm 132:17–18).

In the Old Testament, God fought for Israel and gained victory for its people. God was their defense (His shield) and offense (His deadly and powerful horn). Horns are emblems of power, dominion, glory, and fierceness; they are the chief means of attack and defense. The expression "horn of salvation" applied to Christ, a strong Savior.

> Blessed be the Lord God of Israel; for he hath visited and redeemed his people, And hath raised up an horn of salvation for us in the house of his servant David. (Luke 1:68–69)

The Amplified Bible translates "horn of salvation" as "a mighty and valiant Helper, the Author of salvation." The horn of salvation is the Messiah, the resurrected Lord Jesus of David's lineage.

The apostle Paul wrote,

> You see, at just the right time, when we were still powerless, Christ died for the ungodly. Very rarely will anyone die for a righteous man, though for a good man someone might possibly dare to die. But God demonstrates his own love for us in this: While we were still sinners, Christ died for us. (Romans 5:6–8 NIV)

God used His power to rescue those who had no power to save themselves from sin. When Zechariah said God "has raised up a horn of salvation for us," he meant God would use His incomparable power to save us. There is no power that can prevent God from saving us.

36. Jehovah-M'Kaddesh—Sanctifier

> And ye shall keep my statutes, and do them: I am the
> LORD who sanctify you. (Leviticus 20:8)

To sanctify means commonly to make holy, that is, to separate from the world and consecrate to God. The word that is used here in the name M'Kaddesh has at its root the Hebrew word *kadash* or *kadosh,* "to consecrate, sanctify, prepare, dedicate, be hallowed, be holy, be sanctified." The primary meaning of the word is to set apart or separate. So sanctification or holiness has two meanings—to set apart from sin, and to set apart for God. If you belong to God, you shouldn't live like others; you should be sanctified, set apart from the world, sin, and the flesh.

Only God is holy. He calls us to be holy like Him. He will transform us. Butterflies start off as caterpillars; a metamorphosis occurs in their cocoons; they are totally transformed. Likewise, God wraps us in the cloak of His holiness until we are totally transformed into something we could not be except for Him and His great grace. He shares His character and nature with us through Jesus Christ.

> The Lord says: "Sanctify yourselves therefore, and be
> holy, for I am the Lord your God. And you shall keep my
> status, and perform them: I am the Lord that sanctifies
> you." (Leviticus 20:7–8 NKJV)

37. Jehovah Mgaddishcem— The Lord Our Sanctifier

> And I will sanctify the tabernacle of the congregation,
> and the altar: I will sanctify also both Aaron and his sons,
> to minister to me in the priest's office. (Exodus 29:44)

To separate from the world is to consecrate unto God. To sanctify anything is to declare it belongs to God. Sanctification is through the redemptive work of Christ and the work of the indwelling Holy Spirit. It begins at regeneration and is completed when we see Christ.

God wants to sanctify us completely in body, soul, and spirit. Jesus tells us He wants us to be perfect just as His Father is. We get three specific things as a result of Jesus dying on the cross for our sins—redemption, righteousness, and sanctification.

Most Christians know about the first two—redemption and righteousness—but they do not pick up on the third thing—our sanctification in the Lord! This sanctification is a progressive work done by the Holy Spirit over the course of our lives.

> To the church of God which is at Corinth, to those who are sanctified in Christ Jesus, called to be saints, with all who in every place call on the name of Jesus Christ our Lord. (1 Corinthians 1:2 NKJV)

> But of Him you are in Christ Jesus, who became for us wisdom from God—and righteousness and sanctification and redemption. (1 Corinthians 1:30 NKJV)

> Now may the God of peace Himself sanctify you completely; and may your whole spirit, soul, and body be preserved blameless at the coming of our Lord Jesus Christ. (1 Thessalonians 5:23 NKJV)

Sanctification in the Lord is done by the power of the Holy Spirit operating through the knowledge of the Word of God.

38. Jehovah Misqabbi—The Lord My High Tower

> I will love thee, O LORD, my strength. The LORD is my rock, and my fortress, and my deliverer; my God, my strength, in whom I will trust; my buckler, and the horn of my salvation, and my high tower. I will call upon the LORD, who is worthy to be praised: so, shall I be saved from mine enemies. The sorrows of death compassed me, and the floods of ungodly men made me afraid. The sorrows of hell compassed me about: the snares of death prevented me. In my distress, I called upon the LORD, and cried unto my God: he heard my voice out of his temple, and my cry came before him, even into his ears. (Psalm 18:1–6)

A high tower is a defense, but it is also a place that affords a great vision. God's vision is impossible for us to comprehend. When the men of Babel wanted to be like God, they tried to build a tower. God reacted to this threat; He frustrated their plan. God confused their languages to confound their efforts. Look around at the horrors science without God has created.

With God providing the high place, with God providing the vision, He shared His vision with the men of the Bible. God told Abraham and Moses of His plans for His people. Jesus spent three years explaining His vision to the disciples. He raised them up. He was a high tower of teaching and vision for them. We need great vision, but it must be vision through God and with God. We all need a place of safety, and we need God's vision for our lives and ministries.

39. Jehovah 'Ori—The Lord My Light

> The LORD is my light and my salvation; whom shall I
> fear? the LORD is the strength of my life; of whom shall
> I be afraid? (Psalm 27:1)

Light represents many things. I will talk on three to cast light on the
significance of the name Jehovah-Ori.

1. Protection

Light provides protection; it causes darkness to flee. We turn on lights
to do that, and we build campfires to spot wild animals—dangers.

2. Inspiration

Light is commonly associated with inspiration. The name Jehovah-
Ori carries inspirational significance.

3. Direction

Light is also indicative of direction. Psalm 119:105 says, "Thy Word
is a lamp unto my feet, and a light unto my path." Light gives us the
right direction to go. Jehovah-Ori provides that direction by leading us
through the truth of His Word. Light makes vision possible. Without
light, we are blind. The absence of sunlight causes blindness. Animals
that live in complete darkness are commonly blind.

The Lord is our protection and our inspiration who fills us with
wisdom from on high. He's our guidance as we walk through this world.
The Lord is our light.

We are to let our light shine to expose the darkness of others. I believe
that if people could see more Christians, there would be more Christians.

Before Jesus, most of the world was spiritually blind because they had
rejected God. Humanity was spiritually blind and therefore spiritually
lost. Jesus came as light to help the world regain its sight. Jesus said in
John 12:35 (NKJV), "He who walks in darkness does not know where
he is going." He said in John 12:46 (NKJV), "I have come as light into

the world, that whosoever believes in Me should not abide in darkness."
He said in John 9:39 (NKJV), "I come into this world, that those who do
not see may see."

40. Jehovah Yasha—The Lord Thy Savior

> And I will feed them that oppress thee with their own flesh; and they shall be drunken with their own blood, as with sweet wine: and all flesh shall know that I the LORD am thy Savior and thy Redeemer, the mighty One of Jacob. (Isaiah 49:26)

This Great Salvation

> How shall we escape if we neglect so great a salvation, which at the first began to be spoken by the Lord, and was confirmed to us by those who heard Him. (Hebrews 2:3)

Every one of us begins life with a natural birth. Jesus referred to this birth as being "born of water." Through Adam, sin entered this world; humanity was separated from God and needed a Savior—Jesus.

Salvation is for everyone; 2 Peter 3:9 tells us, "The Lord is not slack concerning His promise, as some count slackness, but is longsuffering toward us, not willing that any should perish but that all should come to repentance."

Salvation comes through the blood of Jesus Christ. Under the old covenant, salvation came through the sacrificial blood of lambs and goats; in the new covenant, it came through Jesus's blood sacrifice. Hebrews 9:22 (NKJV) tells us, "And according to the law almost all things are purged with blood, and without shedding of blood there is no remission." This is why Jesus Christ is the only way for our salvation; His shed blood atoned for our sin.

Jesus is the only way to salvation. Acts 4:12 tells us,

> Neither is there salvation in any other, for there is no other name under heaven given among men by which we must be saved.

Hebrews 9:13–16 reads,

> For if the blood of bulls and goats and the ashes of a heifer, sprinkling the unclean, sanctifies for the purifying of the flesh, ow much more shall the blood of Christ, who through the eternal Spirit offered Himself without spot to God, cleanse your conscience from dead works to serve the living God. And for this reason He is the Mediator of the new covenant, by means of death, for the redemption of the transgressions under the first covenant, that those who are called may receive the promise of the eternal inheritance. For where there is a testament, there must also of necessity be the death of the testator.

Salvation is a gift from God to us. Ephesians 2:8–9 (NKJV) reads,

> For by grace you have been saved through faith, and that not of yourselves; it is the gift of God, not of works, lest anyone should boast.

Salvation has nothing to do with whether we deserve it. It is not based on how good we are or have been; it's based on our belief in Jesus Christ. Romans 10:9–10 (NKJV) reads,

> That if you confess with your mouth the Lord Jesus and believe in your heart that God has raised Him from the dead, you will be saved. For with the heart one believes to righteousness, and with the mouth confession is made to salvation.

Salvation is much more than just being saved from hell and going to heaven. It involves every aspect of our lives—spirit, soul, and body. When we are born again by God's Spirit, we become partakers of His divine nature, which brings us a rich inheritance.

The Greek words for "saved" and "salvation" are *sozo* and *soteria*, which mean to save, deliver, protect, heal, preserve, to do well, be or make whole, and rescue or safety.

God's Grace

Many of us fail to walk in the fullness of God's grace and thus walk in a spirit of condemnation and guilt. Galatians 3:3 (NKJV) asks us, "Are you so foolish? Having begun in the Spirit, are you now being made perfect by the flesh?" If you knew you had only one month to live, how would you prepare to meet the Lord? Would you pray harder? Would you read your Bible more? Would you become more involved in spiritual works? Would you give more money? Would you witness to everyone you saw? If your answer was yes to these questions, you're a performance-based Christian trying work to gain God's favor. But there is no amount of work you could do to earn any more of God's favor. His grace is a gift. Are you living by grace or by performance?

> For by grace you have been saved through faith, and that not of yourselves; it is the gift of God, not of works, lest anyone should boast. For we are His workmanship, created in Christ Jesus for good works, which God prepared beforehand that we should walk in them." Grace is God's free and unmerited favor shown to guilty sinners who deserve only judgment. The love of God shown to the unlovely. God reaching downward to people who are in rebellion against Him. "Being confident of this very thing, that He who has begun a good work in you [by His grace] will [will also by His grace] complete it until the day of Jesus Christ. (Ephesians 2:8–10 NKJV)

Hell

A certain Richman who was clothed in purple and fine linen. But there was A certain beggar named Lazarus full of sore 's, who was laid at his gate, desiring to be feed with the crumbs which fell from the rich man's table. Moreover, the dogs came and licked his sores. (Dogs showed more compassion) So it was the beggar died, and was carried by the Angels to Abrahams bosom. The Richman also died and was buried. And being in torments in Hades, he lifted up his eyes and saw Abraham afar off, and Lazarus in his bosom. Then he cried and said, Father Abraham, have Mercy on me, and send Lazarus that he may dip the tip of his finger in water and cool my tongue, for I am tormented in this flame. But Abraham said son, remember that in your lifetime you received good things, and Lazarus evil things; but now he is Comforted, and you are Tormented. And besides all this, between us and you there is a great gulf fix, so those who would pass from here to you cannot, nor can those from there pass to us. (Luke 16:19–26 NKJV)

He opens his eyes and sees he is in hell, a torment, rather than heaven, a comfort. Hell is a place of weeping, wailing, and gnashing of teeth. Death is not the end of your problems; it's only the beginning if you end up in hell. People today who commit suicide are saying, "If I take my life, it will be all over." But that only opens the door to eternal torments.

The rich man could talk, see, reason, and remember. He was in a dreadful place with no escape. Religions teach that you can pray your way out, but that's not possible. The man Jesus was referring to is still there and will always be there no matter how much he pleads and begs.

Hell is a place of separation from God. When your friends turn from you, that hurts deeply, but nothing will hurt you more than when you can see God and heaven but He doesn't see you. The rich man would have given all he had not to go there. Why do people neglect salvation? What shall it profit those to gain the world but lose their souls?

Hell is not like touching a hot stove that will burn you temporarily; it's an eternal fire where, Jesus said, "the worm never dies." The worms and the fire will eat at you forever.

"War is hell," some have said. But war doesn't even touch what hell is. Wars end, but hell never does. There's no nightmare like the one from which you will never wake up.

No one really plans on going to hell. Some rebellious types will tell you, "I have a lot of friends there." According to the scriptures, it was prepared for the devil and his angels. If you or I go there, we're trespassing. God didn't intend for us to go there, but we're warned it exists.

The rich man had the same opportunity as we do to be saved: life or death, heaven or hell. It's our choice. It doesn't matter how religious we think we are; it depends on our relationship with Jesus Christ.

> Then he said, I beg you therefore, father, that you would send him to my father's house, for I have five brothers that he may testify to them, lest they also come to this place of torment. Abraham said to them, they have Moses and the prophets; let them hear them. And he said, no father Abraham; but if one goes to them from the dead, they will repent. But he said unto them, if they do not hear Moses and the prophets, neither will they be persuaded though one rise from the dead. (Luke 16:27–31 NKJV)

What's going on in hell right now? They're praying. They're praying their loved ones don't end up there. They never got down on their knees to pray before, but they're praying now. Some of us think we can survive without prayer, but even our Savior had to pray. If we think we're going to heaven and never pray, we better be careful.

Nowhere in the Word is it said that the rich man prayed until he went to hell. He never looked to God, never said there was a God. In hell, he prayed, but it was too late. Prayers said in hell aren't answered.

The Rich Man Prays too Late

There are two places where people pray—this world and hell. Those who do not pray here will pray for a Savior in hell. The first time the rich man had a need for a Savior was in hell; he had had no time for religion on earth, but he did in hell. He prayed for mercy, for water, but there is no water in hell. Have you ever been thirsty? He prayed that someone be sent to preach to his brothers. He prayed, "Lord, send them to my father's house. Send someone to my five brothers to testify to them of this place. Don't let them come here." But his prayers weren't answered. There is no pardon in hell. There is no escape. You're locked away and will never have a lawyer to plead your case or judge to change your sentence. A governor might pardon some on death row, but once people are in hell, no judge will let them out.

A man had a dream of Judas in hell. He said, "I don't know why God let me see that, but I saw it." He said he saw Judas in a dry riverbed trying to get water. He was scrubbing his hands. In the vision, he asked, "What are you doing?" Judas asked, "Can't you see it? That's the blood of Jesus. I betrayed Him, and now I'm trying to get His blood off my hands. But I can't. It won't come off. Help me get it off!"

How many of us could end up in that same riverbed because we have spoken badly of our neighbors or have murdered our brothers and sisters with our tongues? We've held the church back from growing. God never intended for the church to put on the brakes; He never intended for people to work against the ministry. The reward for that is hell.

Some of you may have lost the real reason for coming to church. You lost the purpose of serving God, and your joy and peace are gone, but God wants to restore your life and keep you from hell. God doesn't send people to hell; people choose to send themselves there.

Hell is a place of

- no rest day or night (Revelation 14:10)
- wailing and gnashing of teeth (Matthew 13:42)
- unquenchable fire (Mark 9:43)
- full consciousness (Luke 16:25)
- torment (Luke 16:23)
- regret (Luke 16:25)
- separation from God but not from misery and pain (Luke 16:19–26)
- frustration and anger (Matthew 13:42)
- fire that does not consume (Luke 16:22)

- so terrible that those who are there plead for ways of warning others about it (Luke 16:27)
- everlasting punishment (Matthew 25:46)
- everlasting fire (Jude 1:7)
- eternal damnation (Mark 3:29)
- vengeance of eternal fire (Jude 1:7)
- shame and everlasting contempt (John 5:28)
- torment day and night (Revelation 20:10)
- where their worm does not die and the fire is not quenched (Mark 9:44)

An Atheist and Billy Graham

An atheist said to Billy Graham, "Mr. Graham, you really have played the fool all your life about this God stuff. You've talked about heaven and its beauty, but there is no heaven or hell. We're just a bunch of animals, and when we breathe our last, we have nobody to answer to. Why are you preaching this junk?"

Billy Graham said, "I want to tell you something, sir. There is a heaven, and there is a God, and there is a hell, but there is also salvation. If you're right, I haven't lost anything. I have enjoyed my life, and it has been good to be good, and it has been pleasant to dwell among pleasant people. So I haven't lost anything if that's all there is. But if you're wrong, you have really lost and I am going to be the winner. I am going to win because I know the Word of God is true. There is a hell to stay away from, a heaven to gain, and a Savior to rejoice in."

> I am he that liveth, and was dead, and, behold, I am alive forevermore, amen, and have the Keys of Hell and Death. (Revelation 1:18)

Who reading this really wants to go to hell? Is there anybody? Nobody will raise his or her hand. No one wants to go there.

III. The Name of God Almighty—El Shaddai— Almighty God

> The Lord said to Abram, I AM Almighty God-El Shaddai. I will multiply you exceeding ... I will make you exceedingly fruitful. I AM the God that pours out blessings. (Genesis 17:1, 2, 6)

The Hebrew word *shad* means breast, so *shaddai* means primarily "the breasted one." Shaddai is the nourisher, the strength giver, the satisfier. In Hebrew, shaddai means the all-sufficient one, the one who is more than enough. It also means mountain. El-Shaddai is our nourisher, our strength giver, our satisfier. He makes us fruitful and multiplies us exceedingly. Throughout the Old Testament, almighty God revealed himself as El-Shaddai, the God who is more than enough.

David's Mighty Men

We read about David's mighty men of war and think we're reading some kind of superhero comic book. One killed 800 of the enemy, and another killed 300. They did supernatural things because the power of God, which was more than enough, was upon them even in war.

Jesus and a Boy's Lunch (John 6:9)

After the Sermon on the Mount, the people had been without food for several days. They looked around and all they found was a little boy who offered his lunch—five loaves and two fish. Jesus fed at least 5,000 with that. He is the God who is more than enough.

A preacher once said that that wasn't a miracle, that the loaves of bread were bigger in those days. He was forgetting it was just a boy's lunch. The kid would have had to have been carrying two whales and the Pillsbury Doughboy in his pocket to feed that many.

Jesus will take what you give Him—your time, talent, money—and will bless it and multiply it. Give and it shall be given to you. Twelve loaves were given back to him.

The Wedding in Cana (John 2:5)

Jesus told servants to fill the pots with water and take them to the master of the feast. They did, and the water had been turned to wine. The master said, "You have saved the best till last." He is the God who is more than enough.

Lazarus (John 11:25)

After Lazarus dies, Jesus goes to his home. Martha greets Jesus with, "If you had been here, my brother would not have died."

Jesus said, "I am the resurrection and the life." There is no such thing as an impossible situation with God—even death. No matter what you need, He is all sufficient yesterday, today, and forever.

God does not know defeat. If your situation is hopeless, He is the God of hope. Someone said, "How great it will be someday." But things can be great right now. God is the God of now. He's what you need right now. You'll know no lack. He's always more than enough.

In Psalm 91:14–16 are seven things El-Shaddai, the God who is more than enough, said He would do for those who loved Him.

1. "I will deliver them."

You may pray, "God, give me strength to go through this trial." He will, but He wants to deliver you through this. Psalm 34:19 reads, "Many are the afflictions of the righteous, but the Lord delivers them from them ALL."

2. "I will set him on high."

And it shall come to pass, if thou shalt hearken diligently unto the voice of the LORD thy God, to observe and to do all his commandments which I command thee this day, that the LORD thy God will set thee on high above all nations of the earth: And all these blessings shall come on thee, and overtake thee, if thou shalt hearken unto the voice of the LORD thy God. Blessed shalt thou be in the city, and blessed shalt thou be in the field. Blessed shall be the fruit of thy body, and the fruit of thy ground, and the fruit of thy cattle, the increase of thy kine, and the flocks of thy sheep. Blessed shall be thy basket and thy store. Blessed shalt thou be when thou comest in, and blessed shalt thou be when thou goest out.

The LORD shall cause thine enemies that rise up against thee to be smitten before thy face: they shall come out against thee one way, and flee before thee seven ways. The LORD shall command the blessing upon thee in thy storehouses, and in all that thou settest thine hand unto; and he shall bless thee in the land which the LORD thy God giveth thee.

The LORD shall establish thee an holy people unto himself, as he hath sworn unto thee, if thou shalt keep the commandments of the LORD thy God, and walk in his ways.

And all people of the earth shall see that thou art called by the name of the LORD; and they shall be afraid of thee. And the LORD shall make thee plenteous in goods, in the fruit of thy body, and in the fruit of thy cattle, and in the fruit of thy ground, in the land which the LORD sware unto thy fathers to give thee.

The LORD shall open unto thee his good treasure, the heaven to give the rain unto thy land in his season, and to bless all the work of thine hand: and thou shalt lend unto many nations, and thou shalt not borrow. (Deuteronomy 28:1–12)

3. "He shall call upon me, and I will answer him."

God always has been a prayer-answering God. All through the Bible, God said, "I will answer thee." Jeremiah 33:3 reads, "Call unto me, and I will answer thee, and shew thee great and mighty things, which thou knowest not." John 16:23 says, "Whatsoever ye shall ask the Father in my name he will give it you. Ask, and ye shall receive that your joy may be full."

4. "I will be with him in trouble."

John 16:33 reads, "Ye shall have tribulation." God did not say you wouldn't have troubles. Jesus said the world would talk about us, persecute us, and speak evil of us. If they hated Him, they will hate us.

But the God who is more than enough delivers us out of all trouble. He is not some fair- weather friend who is there only when good is happening. He's also there in times of trouble.

5. "I will honor him."

I would rather have God's honor than the greatest honor this world could bestow. The world has its favorite politicians, generals, scientists, and movie and rock stars. If the world is going to honor a preacher, he will be one who doesn't believe in the virgin birth or the Word.

The people of this world will find out that we born-again, Spirit-filled, divine-healing folks are the favorites of the King of Kings and Lord of Lords, the apple of His eye. I may never attain fame in this life, but there is one who knows my name—Jesus. One day, He'll confess me before my Father in heaven and all the heavenly host.

Don't seek the fame and honor of this world; seek God, and He will exalt you on high.

6. "With long life, will I satisfy him."

God said, "I will satisfy him with long life!" That's here on earth. "On earth as it is in heaven." Proverbs tells us that doing certain things will add days to our lives. If we don't, that will shorten our lives.

> Forget not my law, but let thine heart keep my commandments; for length of days, and LONG LIFE, and peace, shall they add to thee. (Proverbs 3:1–2)

> Happy is the man who findeth wisdom, and the man that getteth understanding. LENGTH OF DAYS is in her right hand, and in her left-hand riches and honor. (Proverbs 3:13, 16)

Ephesians 6:3 commands us to honor our parents. Paul spoke here of the First Commandment with the promise "that it may be well with you, and thou mayest live long on the earth." Obedience to parents will add days; disobedience to parents will shorten days.

The devil wants children to be disobedient so he can cut their lives short. He will try to instill rebellion in them at their prime. Parents are responsible for their children's obedience; they shouldn't say, "I don't know what to do with them!"

Children, if you're having problems with your parents, I have good news for you—honor your father and mother.

Psalm 90:9–10 talks about three score and ten years—seventy years. People think if you are seventy, you have one foot in the grave and the other on a banana peel. That's all God promises. Moses was saying that because of their disobedience, they would live to only seventy and wander in the wilderness. Beloved, you have not outlived your life at age seventy. God said, "With long life I will satisfy you."

7. "I will show him my salvation."

God says because you have shown your love to Him, He will give you deliverance, safety, preservation, health, and healing.

IV. God the Master Potter

The Word of the Lord which came to Jeremiah from the Lord saying, "Arise, and go down to the potter's house, and then will I cause them to hear my words." (Jeremiah 18:1)

Vessel of Honor

A vessel of honor is one that will give out pure water to quench the thirst of strangers and weary travelers. The mission of a vessel of honor is to freely give water, the gift of God, to passers-by. Matthew 10:8 reads, "Freely ye have received, freely give."

Vessel of Dishonor

This vessel remains at home. All the stale water in the vessel of honor will be emptied into it. It receives but gives out little. Luke 12:48 reads, "For unto whosoever much is given, of him shall much required."

In Jeremiah 22:28, we read of a vessel called "empty of pleasure." This sits beside the vessel of honor on the bench. This vessel receives the leftover water from the vessel of honor. Its insides become slimy and its water smelly; there is no pleasure in it to the potter or the owner. Revelation 3:16 reads, "Because thou art lukewarm, and neither cold nor hot, I will spew thee out of my mouth."

Isaiah 5:6 tells us, "I got a song to sing about my best friend God." God had a vineyard that He gave special treatment; it was a fertile hill that grew the choicest vines. He took out stones from it and built a watchtower. He waited for harvest time, but it produced worthless grapes. "I will lay it waste. It shall not be pruned. There shall come up briers and thorns."

John 15:2 tells us, "Every branch in me that beareth not fruit he taketh away; and cast into the fire. And every branch that beareth fruit, he purgeth it that it may bring forth more fruit."

Being Tested

No pain, no gain. A woman once said she never had any trouble as a Christian; the devil never bothered her. I didn't believe that. Two cars going in the same direction will never crash head-on. We serve a sovereign God, and we will be tested. If we're never tested, we better check what direction we're heading. We're not tempted by God to do wrong, but we are tested by God to become stronger.

There was a test once done with cocoons. They cut a large hole at the end of some of the cocoons. They found that the ones that had to cut their own way out immediately developed the ability to fly. Those that had had it easy never got off the ground. Struggling will make you strong. But it seems every time a trial comes our way we get angry with God. We quit going to church and stop tithing.

God loves you; that's why you're being tested: God knows you have what it takes. He knows what you're made of. He wouldn't let the devil come against you just to see you fall.

Drying Stage

Wet clay is set on a shelf to dry out with other vessels; it is a testing time. The Lord placed you on the shelf to dry, and for the first time, you feel the scorching desert winds. It doesn't take long after you have been saved for the testing to come. You cry out, "Lord, I'm afraid. The winds are so hot." At first, you assume it won't last long. But after a month, you say, "Lord, I've been setting on this shelf for a long time. Where are you? I can't feel your presence. Are you even close by?" That happened to me for six months until I learned that we walk by faith, not by sight, that the just shall live by faith, not feelings.

When He sits you on the shelf and the desert winds blow against you, there's a transformation taking place. You're getting stronger as you go through the heat.

Jesus Tempted in the Wilderness

The Bible says, "Jesus was led up of the Spirit into the wilderness to be tempted of the Devil." It didn't say that the Lord tempted him. "And when Jesus had fasted 40 days He hungers. The tempter came to Him and said, 'If thou be the Son of God command these stones be made bread.'"

The devil won't come at you when you feel you can move mountains; he'll come when you're weak, when you feel the desert winds blowing against you.

The devil came and said, "If thou be the Son of God ..." The Greek says, "You are the Son of God, turn these stones into bread." So here comes the devil saying, "I know you're hungry." The devil knows when you're weak. He pointed to some stones and told Jesus, "All you have to do is speak to these stones and they will be turned to bread." Jesus said, "It is written, man shall not live by bread alone, but by every word that proceeded out of the mouth of God."

The Bible says the devil took Jesus to a pinnacle of the temple and said, "You, the Son of God, cast yourself down. You know what the scripture says: 'He shall give his angels charge over the, and in thy hands, they shall bear thee up least at any time thou dash thy foot against a stone.'" But Jesus would not jump. He would have had throngs of people follow Him like Superman. Jesus would not bow down to the temptation of Satan.

The devil said, "Look, Son of God. Every direction that you can look, all these cities as they shine before you. I'll give every one of them to you if you will fall down and worship me." Jesus said, "Get thee hence, Satan: For it is written, 'Thou shalt worship the Lord thy God, and him only.'"

God led His Son into the wilderness to be tested. You as a vessel will be tested. But there's coming a promotion if you speak the Word of God and worship and serve Him in the bad times as well as the good times.

> God led thee 40 years in the wilderness, to humble thee, and to prove thee, to know what was in thine heart, whether thou wouldest keep his Commandments or not. He humbled thee and suffered thee to hunger, and fed thee with manna, that HE MIGHT MAKE THEE KNOWN that man doth not live by bread only, but by

every WORD THAT PROCEEDETH OUT OF THE
MOUTH OF LORD. (Deuteronomy 8:2–3)

Job

Job 1:7 reads, "THE Lord said unto Satan, whence comes thou? From going to and fro in the earth, and from walking up and down it," in other words, "seeking whom I may devourer." The devil wants to bring you down, but Jesus has confidence in you. He knows you can stand the test, the heat, and the fire. God said, "Have you considered my servant Job?" The devil said, "I have my eye on him, but I can't get to him. There's a hedge around him, his house, and his family. The only reason Job is serving you is because you're blessing him. (Many serve God only because He's blessing them). If you take away what he has, he won't serve you."

God said, "Go." A servant told Job that everything he had had was gone. His wife tells him, "Job, why don't you just curse God and die?" Now that's encouraging!

Then he gets three church members (devils in the flesh) who sit down in front of him for seven days and don't say anything.

If I'm ever lying in a hospital bed, don't come and just sit down and look at me.

When they finally open up their mouths, they said, "Job you did something wrong. You haven't been living right." Yet the Bible says he was a just man who showed no evil.

I wonder how many today if they lost everything including their children would not backslide. How many of them could say, "Praise the Lord!" during such testing?

Job said, "Naked I came into this world, and naked shall I return. Blessed be the name of the Lord." That didn't work. The devil wanted another try at him. "If you let me have his flesh, he will curse you to your face." "Go," God said, "but do not kill him." The devil ran out of there like a whirlwind after Job and inflicted him with boils all over his body.

The Bible says he took broken pieces of pottery and carved into his body to bring relief, but he never cursed God. If you stay faithful to God, he will give you a promotion. The Lord gave Job twice as much as he had before.

We are in the hands of a sovereign God. Many of us play religion; we think we're coming back next Sunday and will straighten things out then. God says, "I will take you off the shelf and put you on your back so you can hear what I am trying to say to you." God allowed Job to be struck with boils, and there was no relief until the hand of God moved.

David

In Psalm 23, David wrote, "He maketh me to lie down." You have to interpret it this way. "God knocked David flat on his back." David committed adultery and murder, and the Lord knocked him flat on his back. While he was in that position, God could talk to him. Is that what God will have to do to you?

In the Hands of the Master Potter—Shattered

Jeremiah was known as the weeping prophet, but we're living in a time that says we can't weep. It's a weakness in men. If you think this, you're wrong; God says you are to be broken to shed tears of compassion, joy, and love. Jeremiah was to give a message to Israel and every follower of God.

> Arise, and go down to the potter's house, and there I will cause thee to hear my words. Then I went to the potter's house, and, behold he wrought a work on the wheels. And the vessel that he made of clay was MARRED in the hand of the potter: So, he made it again another vessel, as seemed good to the potter to make it. Then the Word of the Lord came to me saying O house of Israel, cannot I do with you as this potter? Saith the Lord. Behold, AS THE CLAY IS IN THE POTTERS HAND, SO ARE YOU IN MY HAND, O HOUSE OF ISRAEL. (Jeremiah 18:2–6)

When Jeremiah was watching the potter, the vessel was marred in his hands, but "He made it again into another Vessel, as seemed good to the potter who made it."

Because of some defect in the clay, the potter changed his mind, crushed the jar into a shapeless mass of clay, and fashioned it into a different vessel.

God asks, "Cannot the clay yield to the potter's hand?" It's important that you understand this; it has been ordained that you read this. When you were young, you were like a piece of clay. God was working, shaping, and molding your life. But there is another side of this, about a man's life that was once soft just like clay.

I have heard people say that Judas was a devil from the beginning, but the scripture gives no support to this at all. Clay is pliable when it is wet; it hasn't gone through the fire. The moisture is still there. It feels like it has life; it gives. That's the way Judas was. He was an ordained minister meant to carry out the works of the Lord as were the other eleven disciples. But Judas was called the son of perdition.

Jeremiah said, "God wrought a work on the wheel and the vessel that he made was marred in his hand." It means he wouldn't yield. After God had shaped it, it deformed itself. It became like people's lives. It became hard. Same clay but no moisture. The Master can no longer shape you or move you. A lot of people are like this.

God said my Word is like a hammer; His anointing keeps striking you. Oh, my brother and sister, will you not heed my anointing?

What Happens When It's Marred?

Then Judas, which had betrayed him, when he saw that he was condemned, repented himself, and brought again the thirty pieces of silver to the chief priests and elders, saying, "I have sinned in that I have betrayed the innocent blood." And they said, "What is that to us? See thou to that." And he cast down the pieces of silver in the temple, and departed, and went and hanged himself. And the chief priests took the silver pieces, and said, "It is not lawful for to put them into the treasury, because it is the price of blood." And they took counsel, and

bought with them the potter's field, to bury strangers in.
(Matthew 27:3–7)

Judas was not a devil from the beginning though he was called a son of perdition. He returned the silver and said, "I have betrayed innocent blood." They said, "What is that to us?" The chief priest bought a potter's field, a place of shards, of broken pottery.

I want to prove Judas wasn't a devil from the beginning: "For he was numbered with us, and have obtained part of this ministry" (Acts 1:17). God would not have ordained a devil to carry out His ministry. After Judas returned the money, "Falling headlong, he burst asunder in the midst, and all his bowels gashed out."

What is meant by "son of perdition"? It means wasting something that is precious to Christ. There is a point you can reach where there is no more repairing. If you play church, you'll end up in the potter's field just as Judas did and be a stranger to God. He said to one group, "I don't know you. Depart from me you workers of iniquity."

Peter did the same thing; he also betrayed Jesus. But there was a difference between him and Judas. There was a difference in repentance. The Bible says that Judas repented; all that means is, "I'm sorry I did this. You keep the money." He committed suicide.

Some of us have been around the church so long that there's no moisture in our lives anymore. We really don't care about the anointing, the moisture in our lives. We don't want to be pliable; we don't want to be on God's wheel. We are on a course of our own making.

If you put God first, you will be one of the happiest people in the world. You will have more joy than you will know what to do with. But if you're constantly running from God not wanting to yield to Him, moisture is leaving you. After a while, all He can do is break you into pieces. You can sit in church and become a sherd; you can become broken. When you break God's law, God's law will break you.

God's Law is like this hammer. You can come against it and say, "I'll do my own thing. I'll live as I want to. I don't have to go to church." That's right—you don't have to go to church, and you don't have to pray. But every time you go against the divine laws of God, you're losing moisture.

All people worry about is more money, a better job, a bigger car, a bigger house. Materialism. Temporal things. God's Law says there's more to life than material things. Stop sitting around and wasting your life. You can go through life being stubborn, you can be a wife or a child abuser, you can shack up, you can do whatever you want, but every time you do, God's hammer breaks off a piece of you. You're forming cracks and getting weaker and smaller. Are you being shattered? Is the Spirit of God moving you? That means there's still a little moisture in your life and God is trying to shape you and put you on the potter's wheel.

Maybe you would say, "I'm like Judas. I haven't hung myself, but my life is shattered. I know there was hope when I was young and tender in the Lord, but something happened, and I'm now a marred vessel, I go to church once and a while. But really, I'm not involved anymore."

There was a time when you were pliable. You once sang in the choir. You paid your tithes, and you considered it a joy to testify and to teach Sunday school. You could feel the presence of God from the crown of your head to the soles of your feet.

Is there any hope? Yes. Good news. God can take His hammer and break all the broken pieces of your life into dust. Then He adds water and says, "I'll try one more time."

Simon Peter

Simon Peter was a broken vessel. He had cursed and denied the Lord. But God went to the potter's field and said, "Simon Peter, Satan desires to sift you as wheat, but I prayed for you."

He was out in the potter's field picking up Peter's life. "Simon, you're all still here. You're just shattered." He ground all of Peter's pieces to powder and took him back to the wheel. "Is not my Word like a hammer?" Each blow brings it closer to dust. He adds water. The master is working skillfully with His hammer. He's saying, "Yield to me, my child, once again. This is your second time on the Potter's wheel."

David (Psalm 51:11–12)

David said, "Cast me not away from thy presence" and "return unto me the Joy of thy salvation." There is no joy in being a sherd. There's no joy in being dry or brittle. "I have become a vessel of dishonor, God. Restore unto me the joy of your salvation."

Young People

Young women, listen to me because you may become pregnant the way you play around. Young men, when you get AIDS, we might not be able to lay hands on you to heal you. You're running around behind your parents' backs. You're sneaking around with this one and sleeping with that one. No respect for authority, no respect for your parents.

Let me tell you that you can go to the point of no return. You get to the point where you say, "God, I don't want to hear your voice anymore. I'm going to do my own thing." You're walking on dangerous ground, and you're the biggest fool in school.

When tell the Potter, "I want to be what I want to be," He will let you. The judgment of God might not shatter your vessel today, but you better wake up. Just because you didn't get caught this time or get pregnant that time doesn't mean the next time God will be that merciful. Some say that God no longer deals with them or speaks to them; I say His mercy endures forever, but there comes a time when His judgment will come down.

A Young Man Who Died

A young man was always calling. He didn't want me to pray, and he drank all the time. He had fallen out of a car and had been run over; God was calling him. The hammer struck, but he didn't listen to that strike.

Later on, a gas furnace blew up on him and threw him several feet. That was the second time the hammer of judgment came down. God was trying to say, "Turn your life around!" but he wouldn't listen. He drank for a month and would not eat anything. His liver became like a piece of stone. He chain-smoked, so his lungs were black and he could barely speak.

The hammer of judgment came down on him a third time. One day, I walked in and he was grasping for air. He finally realized he was going to die. He looked at me with tears in his eyes and said, "Pray for me that the Lord will save me now."

I heard Jesus walking through the potter's field picking up every broken piece of this man. All of a sudden, he was soft, pliable piece of clay again.

He told me, "I'm saved now. Everything will be all right."

Three days later, he went to be with the Lord. The Master had come by and had made him whole again. He wasn't marred or cracked anymore.

Do you want to be soft again and on the Potter's wheel, or do you want His judgment to continue to fall on your life? Do you want to be free and no longer shattered or marred? If so, look up to the Lord and say, "Lord, I'm ready. I'm in the Potter's field. Just give me another chance."

God says the requirements are the same as the first time—repent, not say, "I'm sorry" but then do the same thing that got you into that dry state.

You hear the feet of the Master in the Potter's field coming closer to your broken vessel. A strange feeling takes hold of you. He picks up all the pieces—resentment, adultery, malice, strife, all works of the flesh—and grinds them to powder.

Vessel of Mercy

Romans 9:23 reads, "And that he might make known the riches of his glory on the Vessels of Mercy, which he had afore prepared with glory."

As a Christian, you are called out of spiritual deadness and sinful darkness by God's mercy. We are vessels of mercy. We are to focus on this and "Go and make disciples."

V. God Likes You

Some of us may perceive God as a mean and cruel person who wants to punish us for every wrong we do' others see Him as primarily a forgiving God. How you perceive God's actions and thoughts toward you will affect how you relate to Him. Therefore, we must have a correct biblical view of how God perceives us. Jeremiah 29:11 tells us, "For I know the thoughts that I think toward you, says the LORD, thoughts of peace and not of evil, to give you a future and a hope." And Psalm 139:17 reads, "How precious also are Your thoughts to me, O God! How great is the sum of them!"

The Rejoicing Father

> The Lord your God in your midst, The Mighty One, will save; He will rejoice over you with gladness, He will quiet you with His love, He will rejoice over you with singing. (Zephaniah 3:17 (NKJV)

This is where we have the problem. "Do you have any idea what I've done? There's no way God would rejoice over me. I'm no good."

But "He will quiet you with His love."

You're worrying. You don't know how you'll make it. Things are falling apart. But He will quiet you. His peace passes all understanding.

In the midst of your turmoil, He is saying, "I love you. I am right here with you. I have not left you. I have made a covenant with you through my Son, Jesus. I have taken an oath and have sworn by my name that I will take care of you. I will watch over you and protect you. I'll deliver you." He knows everything about you; He knows ever hair on your head.

"He will rejoice over you with singing."

The word *rejoice* in the Hebrew means to spin around, jump up and down over the influence of a violent emotion. So when God begins to sing over you, He jumps up and down, spins around, rejoices, and sings over you. The joy of the Lord is our strength. Joy is one of the fruits of the Spirit, our spirit. God is a rejoicing God, a dancing God.

This Is What the Father Is Like

> Jesus spoke a parable to them, saying, "What man of you having a hundred sheep, if he loses one of them, does not leave the ninety-nine in the wilderness, and go after the one until he finds it? And when he finds it, he lays it on His shoulder, rejoicing." (Luke 15:3 NKJV)

This is a picture of our heavenly Father, who rejoices. The church should be a rejoicing church thankful for what God has given us, thankful for what God has done for us.

> And when he comes home, he calls together his friends and his neighbors, saying to them, rejoice with me, for I have found my sheep which was lost! I say to you that likewise that there will be more joy in Heaven over one sinner who repents than over ninety-nine just persons who need no repentance. (Luke 15:6)

The moment one person repents, the saints of God in heaven rejoice. I believe every time someone who was lost is found, there is an announcement made in heaven.

> Or what women, having ten silver coins, if she loses one coin, does not light a lamp and seek diligently till she finds it? (Luke 15:8)

I believe Jesus is giving us a revelation of His heavenly Father here. He sweeps the house and searches until He finds the missing person and rejoices. He will never give up on you. Jesus said this was what His Father is like: "For I have found the piece which I lost!"

> There is joy in the presence of angels of God over one sinner who repents. (Luke 15:10)

God does not tell the angels to be quiet; the moment a sinner repents, He jumps and spins around. The Bible says it's like a violent emotion that takes over.

In Luke 15:20–22 (NKJV), God is represented by the father figure who was awaiting his son's return, the son who had spent his inheritance on prodigal living. After losing his wealth, he was abandoned by his friends. He was finally given a job caring for pigs.

The father sees him returning, runs to him, and embraces him though by law, the father could have stoned him to death because his son had embarrassed him.

> He arose and came to his father. But when he was still a great way off, his father saw him and had compassion and ran and fell on is neck and kissed him. And the son said to him, "Father, I have sinned against heaven and in your sight, and am no longer worthy to be called your son." (Luke 15:20–21)

The father interrupts him and gives an order.

> But the father said to his servant, "Bring out the best robe and put it on him, and put a ring on his hands and sandals on his feet." The father wanted to see him dressed in royalty. (Luke 15:22)

We are God's heirs! We often call out to God our Father acting like servants. But servants of the Father do not call Him "Father"; they serve Him because they are not His children. When we pray to God, we must do so as a son or daughter and heir.

The Brother

The eldest son had stayed home. He did not spend any money though he had right to a double portion for being the oldest son. As children of God, we must understand that it is not enough just to be in the house; we need to experience and enjoy all God offers us.

Jesus, The Good Samaritan

Luke 10:30 tells us, "A certain man went down from Jerusalem to Jericho, and fell among thieves, who stripped him of his clothing, wounded him, and departed, leaving him half dead." The man represents us before we were saved, when we were naked and half-dead. The thief represents Satan, who comes to kill and destroy.

No name, no culture, was given about this man; the assumption is that he was a Jew whose journey began seventeen miles back. The road he was taking was frequently traveled by priests, Levites, and bandits; it was known as the Bloody Way or the Road to Hell.

He had been stripped of everything he had and had been beaten and left half-dead.

> Now by chance, A Certain Priest came down that road.
> And when he saw him, he passed by on the other side.
> Likewise, a Levite, when he arrived at the place, came
> and looked, and passed by on the other side. (Luke 10:31)

The priest and the Levite represent the Law, which could do nothing; it showed no mercy or compassion. Here was this Priest, a Jew, and here was another Jew, who was moaning and asking for help. But the priest kept on walking; he acted as if the man wasn't there.

A Levite, a person who assisted the priest (a deacon), sees the man but also does nothing; he had no compassion.

We shouldn't be too quick to judge; every day, we are surrounded by people who are going to bell, but we do nothing.

The priest and the Levite represent the dispensation of the Law; they did not show any mercy or compassion.

What was the purpose of the Law? Galatians 3:24 says, "Wherefore the Law was our schoolmaster to bring us unto Christ, that we might be Justified by Faith." It pointed to Calvary. It was our schoolmaster. It pointed to Christ. Man, realizing he is a sinner condemned to die, realizes he needs a Savior.

The Good Samaritan

> But a certain Samaritan, as he journeyed, came where he was. And when he saw him, he had compassion on him, and went to him and bandaged (bound) his wounds, pouring on oil and wine, and he set him on his own animal, brought him to an inn, and took care of him.
>
> On the next day, when he departed, he took out two denarii, gave them to the innkeeper, and said to him, "Take care of him; and whatever more you spend, when I come again, I will repay you." (Luke 10:33–35)

The Samaritan Was a Type of Christ

Jews and Samaritans racially did not get along; they were alienated. The Jews called them dogs. But this Samaritan showed compassion. He looked through the same eyes that Jesus would have looked through. He pushed all this aside and said, "He is my neighbor." That could have been me.

We're looking at the prettiest picture of salvation when he knelt beside him and he poured in the oil and the wine.

Wine—Sanctification

The wine was a disinfectant; we call it sanctification. He began to pour that wine in the man's wounds to kill any infection. That wine wipes away our sins and purifies us.

Oil—Sealed with the Spirit

He poured in the oil of the Spirit so nothing else could get in the wounds. He poured the sealing of the Spirit. We are sealed with the Spirit; the oil of joy refreshes and restores the soul.

Bound It—Identity

After he poured in the oil and the wine on the wounds, he bound them. That was identity. When people saw this man who had been left for dead, they smelled the wine that had purified him and the oil that had sealed his wounds. They could see that someone had helped him and had raised him from the dead.

Sat Him on His Own Beast

This man was saying, "What is mine is yours." They became brothers. When you are saved and sanctified and full of the Spirit, the Lord gives everything He has to you.

Brought Him to an Inn

The Good Samaritan took the man to an inn, a place of safety. We're under the shelter of the wings of the almighty God. The angels of the Lord are encamped around those who fear Him.

Left Him a Promise

The Samaritan said, "Take care of him. If it costs you more, I'll pay you when I come back." I will pay you back for all the good that you have done.

God Loves Us Even in Our Darkest State

Romans 5:8 (NKJV) tells us, "But God demonstrates His own love toward us, in that while we were still sinners, Christ died for us." God the Father couldn't love us any more than He does. He doesn't love us more when we are good, nor does He love us any less when we are bad. Nothing we can do will make God love us more. He loves us as much as He loves His Son, Jesus. Jesus said in John 15:9 (NKJV), "As the Father loved Me, I also have loved you; abide in My love."

VI. Who Will Pray for the Peace of Jerusalem?

Israel is the one nation of the world that is targeted by twenty-two other nations, by four major world empires, and by every major superpower in the world besides the United States. It is surrounded by twenty-two nations that want to give it a 9/11 every day.

Islam says, "We will kill you." Iran says, "You have no right to exist." The United Nations tell them to give back the land they won even though they had been attacked.

Yet almighty God says, "I chose a nation to show my power. Not America, which is the wealthiest nation in the world. Not Russia, which has 27,000 nuclear bombs and 600 arms factories. Not China, which has close to 2 billion people. Not Japan, which has the technology of the world."

God chose Israel, the most threatened, dispersed, attacked, and oppressed nation of the world. God has chosen the nation other nations want to divide, a people almost everybody hates. God says, "By this, I will show the world that I am the King of Kings and the Lord of Lords."

There are 10,396 verses of prophecy in the Bible, and every one of them depends on Israel being a nation, Jerusalem being its capital, and the Jews being back in their land.

There are 613 laws of which you know only ten. Two hundred and sixty-two of them depend on Israel rebuilding the temple. But that's the Law. If you wipe out Israel, if you divide up Jerusalem as one of our presidents wanted to do, if you push the Jewish people into the Red Sea, you will make God a liar and the Word of God a lie.

Why is Israel is under attack by so many nations? It has no gold, silver, brass, iron, or oil—no natural resources. But it is the most coveted piece of property in the world. Satan hates Jerusalem; if he can take Jerusalem, he can turn the Bible into a lie.

This Is What the Devil Would Like

Here comes the devil. "I'll show God. I can't kill him, but I can kill them." He raised up Hitler and killed 6 million Jews, two out of three in Europe. He raised up Stalin and killed another million. The devil thought, "If I can destroy them, if I can scatter them all around the world, if I can destroy their city, God will be a liar."

> Who has heard such a thing? Who has seen such a thing?
> Shall the earth be made to give birth in one day? Or shall
> a nation be born at once? For as soon as Zion travailed,
> she gave birth to her children. (Isaiah 66:8)

When he looked to Israel, he couldn't believe God could raise its people. But let me tell you what the almighty God did—He walked into a bone yard that contained the bleached bones of Israel and said, "I'm not just going to raise you; I'll do so in one day."

> Therefore prophesy and say unto them, thus saith the
> Lord God: Behold, O my people, I will open your graves,
> and cause you to come up out of your graves, and bring
> you into the land of Israel. (Ezekiel 37:12)

The graves of Israel are the nations of the world. God said He would open their graves. That means the nations of the world will have to surrender to it. I am saying to you whatever has buried you, it will have to give you up in the name of Jesus. It cannot bind you, it cannot imprison you, it cannot entomb you anymore. A miracle is about to happen: "I will cause you to come up out of your graves." How many of you are willing to come out of your graves? I have news for somebody—someone is coming out.

America and Israel are the only two nations of the world God connected by the hip. Did you know that Thomas Jefferson wanted the seal of America to be the Jews leaving Egypt? Did you know that Abraham Lincoln wanted the seal to be Moses holding the Ten Commandments? Did you know on our Liberty Bell there is an Old Testament scripture, Leviticus 25:10: "Proclaim liberty through all the earth."

Did you know that America's documents—the Bill of Rights, Declaration of Independence, and Constitution—are built on the five books of Moses and the four gospels? We are the only Judaic-Christian nations in the world.

Prophetic Information

Israel and America came out of other nations. Israel came out of Egypt, and we came out of Israel. Both came out of bondage. They came out of Pharaoh's bondage, and we came out of religious bondage. One was seeking the Promised Land; the other was seeking a land of worship. Israel journeyed by faith, and we journeyed by faith. They were trusting God; we were trusting God. America's founders came under divine inspiration; they also came by divine inspiration. A sea separated them—the Red Sea; an ocean separated us—the Atlantic.

May 14 is significant to them; that was when their nation was rebirthed. May 14 is significant for us. On that date in 1607, our first colony was planted.

The United States and Israel are the only two nations of the world that were divided between the north and the south and fought each other. The tribe of Levi comprised thirteen tribes; we had thirteen colonies. Jerusalem was finished for Israel's second king, King David. Our White House was finished under our second president, John Adams. The only man who ran against Washington was named Israel.

The United States and Israel have been connected for a divine purpose. We have been called in America to be the missionaries to the world and for the defense of Israel. Should America stand with Israel and Jerusalem? Should we tell any president that he cannot divide a city that is holy? It is not his to divide.

On October 30, 1991, President George H. W. Bush convened the Middle East peace treaty in Madrid, Spain. The purpose of the treaty was to convince Israel to give up its land for the peace. The Bible clearly states that Israel is in a covenant with God for this land.

The day that we said for them to give up the promise, a huge storm hit the New England coast; it was called the perfect storm. It was one of the most powerful storms ever. They made a movie and a book about it called *The Perfect Storm*.

On August 23, 1992, the Madrid Peace Conference moved to DC; we were saying, "Give up the Promised Land." On that day, Hurricane Andrew hit Florida.

On September 1, 1993, we were saying, "Give up Gaza," and on that day, Hurricane Emily hit.

On January 16, 1994, President Clinton told the Syrian president Assad to give up the Golan Heights, and on that day, California was rocked by a large earthquake.

On May 13, 1999, Arafat was declaring a Palestinian state with Jerusalem as its capital and we were saying okay; on that day, the most powerful tornado to hit America smashed Oklahoma and Kansas with winds over 300 miles an hour.

In 2008, President George W. Bush was in Israel. He went to Jerusalem, which is called Zion. He was telling them to divide Jerusalem-Zion. That same day, a tornado hit Arkansas in winter. Do you know what city in Arkansas it hit? Jerusalem. Do you know what church it destroyed? Zion.

Condi Rice was in Israel saying give up the West Bank; the West Bank is Judaea and Samaria. The world formed the term *West Bank* to disguise the fact that it is the heartland of Israel. Now, Interstate 10 in Louisiana takes you to the West Bank. The same day, Hurricane Katrina hit.

As efforts are made to remove the land from Israel, there are significant disasters that are occurring often on the very day that they occur.

Calvary, Via Del Rosa, the Mount of Olives, the Temple Mount, Mount Mariah, the Eastern Gate, the Upper Room—who will take a stand for them? Who will say, "We will defend you"? Who will pray for the Peace of Jerusalem?

Here's one more shocking point. Romans 11:17 says, "And some of the branches be broken off, and thou, being a wild olive tree, were grafted in among them, and with them partakest of the root and the fatness of the olive tree." Not all, some. The branches are the Jewish people. They were broken off because they refused to accept the Messiah. Can you tell me who those wild olive trees are? God wanted to fill it back up, so He took us in. We were grafted in among them; they were not grafted in among us. Who is they? The Jews, Israel. So hear this—with them we became partakers of the root.

Olive Tree

You can graft a wild olive tree onto an olive tree, but you can't graft an olive tree onto a wild olive tree. If an olive tree is experiencing trouble, a graft revives it. So when you were grafted, you brought life. But when you were grafted, they gave you covenant blessings so the blessing of Abraham might come upon the Gentiles.

If we are in Christ, we are Abraham's seed, the children of promise. Blessings and covenant breakthroughs are about to come into our lives.

Are You Ready for the Shocker?

When you graft, do you graft from the top, bottom, or side? The graft has to be made from the side. Over two thousand years ago, after He died, that cut had no redemptive value. The shedding of the blood did, but the water didn't. Why did they cut His side? So we could be grafted in.

It takes an olive graft three days and nights to take root. Do you know why healing is coming to somebody? Why prosperity, blessings, and deliverance is coming to somebody? Because his or her graft wasn't authenticated by any preacher or evangelist but by the death, burial, and resurrection of the King of Kings and the Lord of Lords. Can somebody give up praise?

The olive tree is the only tree pollinated by wind. So when the wind of the Holy Spirit is blowing in the church, God is pollinating miracles.

Some of you pray less; you come to church and look like you just drank a bottle of cracker juice. You are so dry while other people are praising and miracles are being pollinated in their lives. You will be left behind in a dry, dreary land.

So church, let the wind blow. Lord, let us preach, let us worship. Lord, let us magnify your name. Wind of God, Spirit of God, blow on us.

Will you make a stand for the land of Israel? For the Jewish people?

Ancient Hatred

Why throughout every generation is the Jew persecuted wherever they live? I can understand why that occurred before the Messiah came. It was from a seed of a Jew that the Messiah would come. But why after? You won't understand the end times unless you understand the Jews and Israel. Even the Jews can't understand this ancient hatred.

Reasons for This Ancient Hatred

There are reasons for the hatred of the Jews in Genesis 3:15, where God said, "And I will put enmity (HATRED) between thee and the woman, and between thy seed and her seed; it shall bruise thy head." Who is He, the Messiah, who will crush the head of the devil? Do you not understand the devil does not want his head crushed?

A Miraculous Sign

Isaiah 7:14 reads, "Therefore the Lord himself will give you a SIGN: (In the Hebrew, the word sign means a miraculous sign, what will this miraculous sign be?) Behold, the virgin shall conceive and bear a son, and shall call his name IMMANUEL." That would be a miraculous sign.

Why doesn't every Jew know Jesus the Messiah? There are three reasons for this.

1. The scriptures say they have spiritual scales on their eyes.
2. They have been taught they cannot be Jews and still believe in Jesus; that's a lie.
3. The Jews have been taught there will be peace when the Messiah comes.

That's in Torah; that is true. But that same Torah is Isaiah 53, which says He will die for our sins. So rather what the ancient rabbis said—two messiahs—that is what the ancient rabbis said. How about one Messiah and two appearances?

The Judgment of God on Israel

The Torah is clear; it says there are judgments for sin. It tells us that the judgment has come, why it will come, and when it will end.

1st judgment: Israel would lose its land.

2nd judgment: Israel would be scattered to the four corners of the earth (they were).

3rd judgment: Jews would be persecuted by every country they went to.

4th judgment: They would be spiritually blind.

Harden the hearts of these people, plug their ears and shut their eyes. That way they will not see with their eyes, nor hear with their ears, nor understand with their hearts and turn to me for healing. (Isaiah 6:10 One New Man Bible)

But I have good news: the judgment is over. The key is found in a phrase that is so important: "the fullness of the Gentiles."

Esther

Esther is a type of the end-time church. Esther, the church, was a young and beautiful orphan. She was a virgin. Let me tell you something, Esther Church—you could have been the biggest streetwalker in town, but when Jesus cleansed you, He made you a virgin.

Esther had favor. She hid the fact that if you are the Messiah's, you are the same as Abraham's seed even though she hid her Jewish roots.

Esther soaked in oil for a year to smell nice for the king. She equipped the Jewish people with the sword, the Word of the Living God. When she reached out to spare the Jewish people, she opened the door for the greatest Gentile revival in history.

Evangelist R. D. Mattock
1eaglesrock@gmail.com

About the Author

Answering my call into the five-fold ministry in 1976. Graduated from Carolina Bible College. Evangelist, Pastor, Teacher. Over forty years Preaching, Teaching, and proclaiming Gods Holy Word. Book is a collection of over 30 sermons that have been preached by myself and others.